THE SUPER
TUTOR

TUTOR

The best education money can buy in seven short chapters

JOE NORMAN

With original illustrations by
George Norman

Published in 2019 by Short Books,
Unit 316, ScreenWorks, 22 Highbury Grove,
London, N5 2ER

10 9 8 7 6 5 4 3 2 1

A CIP catalogue record for this book is
available from the British Library.

ISBN: 978-1-78072-386-0

Cover design by Two Associates

Printed at CPI Group (UK) Ltd, Croydon, CR0 4YY

To William of Wykeham, the founder in 1382 of Winchester College (my metaphorical *alma*[1] *mater*[2]), without which this book would not have been written

And to my literal *alma mater*, Julia Norman, without whom this book would not have been written

---

1 *almus*, *alma*, *almum* (adjective) – nourishing, kind

2 *mater*, *matris* (noun, third declension feminine) – mother

Contents

Introduction 9

1. What to read 21
2. How to read 69
3. How to write 83
4. How to structure an essay 111
5. How to tell a story 163
6. How to understand a poem 185
7. How to avoid common mistakes 241

INTRODUCTION

I don't know why you picked this book up. But you might have noticed that I ended my first sentence with a preposition, 'up', which is supposedly a mistake in good English, and which is 'something up with which I will not put', as Churchill once said.[1] And you may have noticed that I started my second and third sentences with conjunctions, 'But' and 'And'. If you noticed those mistakes and didn't care, or if you didn't notice them at all, this might be the book for you.

Disinterested learning

I first heard the two words that sum up my educational philosophy in 1996, when I was 18, in a speech given by my History teacher Dr Cramer. What was it that made our school – the one we were about to leave after five years – unique, he asked himself? (This school was Winchester College, the oldest of the English public schools.)

[1] Jokingly, because that 'correct' version sounds so much worse than 'something I will not put up with'.

In Dr Cramer's view, what made it unique was this: disinterested learning. The school's ethos was so squarely built on this idea – you should learn something because it's interesting or worthwhile in itself – that we had a lesson every day, called Div in which we'd learn things that had nothing to do with any exam syllabus. There was a weekly essay, a Div Task, which was by far the biggest piece of homework of any given week but which didn't contribute to any exam grade. Nevertheless, coming top of your Div at the end of term was more important than any number of A*s at GCSE.

Disinterested versus uninterested

'Interested' is an odd word. Like 'right', it has two opposites because it has two meanings. When we were younger my brother, if you asked him: 'Are you alright?', was in the habit of replying: 'No, I'm half left'. Because he wasn't all right, only the right side of his body was right. The other half of him was left. He knew 'alright' didn't mean right (= opposite of left) when we asked him; he knew it meant right (= opposite of wrong). He was just being annoying.

Likewise, 'interested' has two antonyms (opposites), because it too has two meanings. The first, usual meaning of interested is keen, avid, fascinated – and its opposite is uninterested, meaning bored, not keen.

But the other, second meaning of interested has to do with money. If you have an interest in a company, you get money from it; if you put your money in a bank, you earn interest on your savings. You might not be super-fascinated by how the company makes the money you get a share of, or by how the compound interest works that makes your savings grow faster than you might expect. You might find that stuff boring – or perhaps just confusing – as hell. But you're still, in the second sense of the word, interested – because you get something out of it. You get interest, or money in some other form. So you're interested, even if you're bored out of your mind by the obscure workings of money.

The opposite of interested, in this secondary sense, is disinterested. Interested parties have something (usually money) to gain. Disinterested parties have nothing to gain, or at least nothing that can easily be measured.

Back to disinterested learning. These days, most people who are up at two in the morning reading Plato have an exam the next day. We don't know whether or not they're interested or uninterested in the primary sense of being fascinated or bored by Greek philosophy. But they're certainly interested in the secondary sense – of having something to gain from reading Plato's Republic as a matter of some urgency.

That looming exam is like money/interest, because you stand to profit from something external or extrinsic to the fun you get from reading a 2400-year-old book about how the world should be run. It might not be money that's at stake

– exam grades are not a hard currency – though of course one of the main reasons people tell you to work hard at school is so you can get a well-paid 'good job' (these '' are called 'scare quotes' by the way, and they indicate a writer's doubt about the idea contained in the phrase they are quoting). But your average late-night Platonist is an interested party – he or she is doing it with a definite goal in view, whether it's getting the 'A' tomorrow or the plush corporate gig in five years.

This attitude towards education can be called instrumentalism – all education, whether you're six or 60, is just an instrument to get you something, whether it's a better job or a place at university, or the opportunity to surprise Hungarians with your fluent Magyar.

Disinterested learning is the opposite of this. You're doing it because it's fun, or worth doing – although, actually, surprising Hungarians probably comes under the category of disinterested learning too, unless it's part of your job description.

I only know four words in Magyar (hello, please, thank you and cheers!). But I did learn Italian after leaving school for no other reason than I decided Italy would be a nice place to go and surprise native speakers. That decision – those hundreds of hours of blathering ineffectually in a foreign language – isn't likely to benefit me financially. I'm not good enough at Italian to teach it, and there's not much call for it anyway. It's just fun to know.

Sprezzatura

The other idea I keep falling back on is *sprezzatura*, an Italian word which means 'studied carelessness' or 'effortless brilliance'. Obviously there's a conflict at this idea's heart – brilliance only comes with care, and study requires effort. It's probably a paradox. For me, the best way of describing *sprezzatura* is with the image of a swan swanning along, its feet beating furiously out of sight, as it glides calmly and gracefully over the surface of the water.

Sprezzatura comes from the 16th-century *Book of the Courtier* by Baldassare Castiglione, which was translated from the original Italian and widely read at the court of Henry VIII. Medieval courts had generally favoured those noblemen who were good at fighting or were born into the most powerful families. But over the centuries the rebirth (Renaissance) of Ancient Greek and Roman learning meant that literacy and wit became more prized. Castiglione's ideal Renaissance Man should be good at everything – especially at things like manners, which it's hard to make rules about, and can't easily be measured or taught. Castiglione coined *sprezzatura* to describe a way of being that acknowledges that some things can't be taught – but that most things can, especially if you don't let on how much effort it took.

Thinking about it, *sprezzatura* isn't far off from the 20th-century idea of 'cool', which comes from Black American culture generally, and jazz music specifically – it was popularised by the jazz saxophonist Lester Young, and suggests a sort of intense, laid-back attitude to music, and to life. Jazz bands don't play songs, they improvise them, so they're constantly thinking mid-piece where it'll go next – but without letting you see them sweat. Miles Davis made an album called Birth of the Cool, and he would know. Nothing effortful here. Just pure cool.

It wasn't cool at Winchester to be seen to be making an effort – is it anywhere? – but it was okay to argue a point compellingly with your teacher, or to come top of your class despite looking like you'd just rolled out of bed.

For my purposes, in my tutorials and in this book, *sprezzatura* means giving the impression that, like an iceberg whose total mass is 90% underwater and invisible, what I'm telling you is just a fraction of what I really know. Whereas the opposite is the truth: I'm frantically scrambling to invert that iceberg, to expose as much as possible of that hidden 90%, the better to suggest even greater hidden depths that aren't really there. It's a kind of showing off, really, but with a purpose, which is to suggest that knowing a lot of apparently unrelated things can be worthwhile in itself – that is, disinterestedly, without anything really at stake. And that – stop the press – it can be fun, too.

Useful or beautiful

I tutor children aged 10-13, almost exclusively, and I don't really worry about their exam results or which famous old schools I succeed or fail to get them into. Their wealthy, educated and highly-motivated parents generally make it impossible for them to really fail. Instead, I worry about what I can teach them that they'll still remember in 30 years, when they're my age. It doesn't even have to be something useful.

William Morris said that you should,

> Have nothing in your home that you neither know to be useful, nor believe to be beautiful.

I believe the same thing is true of our minds. Education doesn't ultimately happen in schools or universities or in the many forms of adult education available, or in public libraries, or even – saints preserve us! – online. Your education happens exclusively in your head, and that will always be true. Who's driving this car? You are.

The contents of this book are largely things I was taught 20-25 years ago, which are still available to me now, because they have stayed with me. Most of the quotations are made from memory. That's the only real criterion for inclusion. Do I still remember it decades later?

Between the chapters I've interpolated a few questions – and answers – that I like to bother my students with. And now I'm bothering you with them. Some are broadly mathematical, some philosophical, and accordingly some have defined answers, while others don't. The point of asking them is not whether you get to the 'right' answer, but that you spend time focusing your intelligence on a narrow point. Skip ahead if you get unpleasantly stuck, though. They're supposed to be fun.

I hope this book will reach not just avid young scholars but also those who are not in formal education any more (of course, your informal education continues throughout your life; perhaps, if you're like me, without you even noticing). What's on offer here is the best academic education available in the English-speaking world, one focused on the intrinsic value of *knowing interesting stuff*,[2] all sifted through the gaping holes of the colander I like to call my mind.

Finally, these chapters should be considered training wheels, to be kicked away when no longer needed. You can read them in any order, dip in and out, or even skip them altogether. One of the things I *am* sure about is that you shouldn't get all your information from one source. Especially if I'm that source.

---

[2] *Interesting* here meaning the opposite of *uninteresting* - i.e. *not boring*.

FIRST QUESTION

THE RIVER PROBLEM

You are a farmer standing on the bank of a fast-flowing river which you need to cross to get home. You have with you a fox, a goose and a sack of beans. You need to transport all three of them across the river, but your rowing boat is small, and you can only take them across one at a time.

There's a further complication. If you leave the fox and the goose together unsupervised, the fox will kill the goose. And if you leave the goose and the beans together, unsupervised, the goose will eat all the beans. You want to avoid both these eventualities while getting the fox and the goose and the sack of beans safely across the river.

How do you do it?

1

WHAT TO READ

Part one: some lists

Here are some lists of some of the books I read between the ages of ten and 40.

Fiction, mostly not funny

1. Paul Biegel - *The King of the Copper Mountains*
2. Roald Dahl - *The Twits* (under 100 pages)
3. Roald Dahl - *The Witches*
4. Roald Dahl - *Boy*
5. Roald Dahl - *Going Solo*
6. Roald Dahl - *The Wonderful Story of Henry Sugar and Six More*
7. EH White - *The Once and Future King* (the first in a series if you finish and still want more)
8. Oscar Wilde - all his children's stories
9. Ted Hughes - *The Iron Man* (under 100 pages)
10. George Orwell - *Animal Farm* (under 100 pages)

11 Gerald Durrell - *My Family and Other Animals* (first in a series)

12 Lewis Carroll - *Alice's Adventures in Wonderland* (the sequel is *Through the Looking Glass*; read both if you're interested in philosophy)

13 Oscar Wilde - *The Picture of Dorian Gray*

14 Armistead Maupin - *Tales of the City* (first in a series)

15 HG Wells - *The Time Machine* (skip to, I think, chapter six, because the first five chapters are HG Wells explaining to his readers what a time machine is, because no one had ever imagined one before)

16 George Orwell - *Down and Out in Paris and London*

17 Jorge Luis Borges[3] - *The Universal Dictionary of Infamy*, or alternatively *Doctor Brodie's Report*[4]

18 Gustave Flaubert - *Three Tales*

19 Donna Tartt - *The Secret History*

20 Robert Louis Stevenson - *Treasure Island*

21 Douglas Adams - *Watership Down*

22 Graham Greene - *The Third Man*

23 Kazuo Ishiguro - *Never Let Me Go*

24 Kazuo Ishiguro - *The Remains of the Day*

---

3 I think the 'J' and both 'G's in his name are pronounced as 'H's in Spanish, though I've heard his name pronounced at least four different ways by knowledgeable people.

4 There are some great podcast readings of Borges stories by famous writers, and they all seem to prefer Norman Thomas di Giovanni's English translations – and so should you.

25 F Scott Fitzgerald - *The Great Gatsby* (maybe my favourite book, as you'll probably twig later; his best short stories are completely brilliant, too)

26 *The Granta Book of the American Short Story* (edited by Richard Ford, the first volume, not the second, which I don't know but is probably excellent too)

27 LP Hartley - *The Go-Between*

28 Jerzy Kosinski - *Being There* and *The Painted Bird*

29 Kurt Vonnegut - *Cat's Cradle*

30 John Wyndham - *The Trouble with Lichen*

31 EM Forster - *The Machine Stops*

32 Jayne Anne Phillips - *Machine Dreams*

33 Harper Lee - *To Kill a Mockingbird*

34 Isabel Allende - *The House of the Spirits*

35 Muriel Spark - *The Prime of Miss Jean Brodie*

36 Barry Hines - *A Kestrel for a Knave* (the Ken Loach film of this book is called simply *Kes*)

37 Carson McCullers - *The Heart is a Lonely Hunter* and *The Ballad of the Sad Café*

38 Mary Shelley - *Frankenstein*

39 Jane Austen - *Pride and Prejudice*

40 Susanna Clarke - *Jonathan Strange and Mr Norrell* (long, but the best fantasy novel I've read)

41 Robert Louis Stevenson - *Dr Jekyll and Mr Hyde*

42 Arthur Conan Doyle - *A Study in Scarlet* (the first Sherlock Holmes story)

43 Daniel Defoe - *Robinson Crusoe*

44 Charles Dickens - *Great Expectations*

45 Laurie Lee - *Cider with Rosie*

46 Jeanette Winterson - *Why Be Happy When You Could Be Normal?* (and her more famous, 'experimental' first novel *Oranges Are Not the Only Fruit*)

47 Lorrie Moore - *The Collected Short Stories*

48 Ursula K. Le Guin - *A Wizard of Earthsea* (see also her version of *Lao Tzu: Tao Te Ching*, a great Chinese classic about power, happiness and the meaning of life)

49 Susan Cooper - *The Dark is Rising* series

50 Vladimir Nabokov - *Lolita*

51 Lionel Shriver - *We Need to Talk About Kevin*

52 VS Naipaul - *The Mimic Men*

53 George Eliot - *Silas Marner*

54 Virginia Woolf - *To the Lighthouse*

55 Michel Houllebecq - *Atomised* (quite recent but feels timeless, if misanthropic)

56 Elena Ferrante - *My Brilliant Friend* (even more recent)

57 Dave Eggers - *A Heartbreaking Work of Staggering Genius*

58 Chinua Achebe - *Things Fall Apart*

59 George Steiner - *The Portage to San Cristobal of A.H.* (about Jewish Nazi-hunters who find Adolf Hitler hiding in the Amazonian rainforest and have to bring him back to civilisation to face justice)

60 Graham Swift - *Waterland*

61 Joseph Conrad - *Heart of Darkness*

62 Arundhati Roy - *The God of Small Things*

Fiction, kind of funny

1 Kenneth Grahame - *The Wind in the Willows*

2 Edward Lear - *The Owl and the Pussycat* (longish poem)

3 Edward Gorey - anything

4 JD Salinger - *The Catcher in the Rye*

5 Julian Maclaren-Ross - *Of Love and Hunger*

6 Charles Bukowski - *Post Office*

7 Nathanael West - *Miss Lonelyhearts* (these last three books are kind of funny about terrible jobs: vacuum cleaner salesman, postman and newspaper agony columnist respectively)

8 Jonathan Swift - *Gulliver's Travels* (skip to the bit when he arrives in Lilliput after the shipwreck as it's a pretty slow start – and if you get bored at any point thereafter, skip to the next of the book's four sections: Gulliver visits four different places – he seems to keep getting shipwrecked, weirdly – but most people don't know the second half of the book at all)[5]

---

[5] There's also a brilliant, short, modern illustrated retelling by Jonathan Coe (called *Gulliver*) for busy people, or for children – although you might be interested to know that George Orwell read the original cover to cover on the day before his eighth birthday (he had hunted down and unwrapped his present while his mother was out of the house), and you can see how the final animal-themed part of Swift's satire influenced young Orwell's *Animal Farm*.

9 Lord Byron - *Don Juan* (an epic comic poem if that's possible, sexy and funny in equal parts. His introduction/dedication is my favourite bit, so just read that and give up if Lord B doesn't satisfy)
10 Mark Twain - *Huckleberry Finn*
11 Laurence Stern - *Tristram Shandy*
12 John Steinbeck - *Tortilla Flat*

Fiction, funny

1 Douglas Adams - *The Hitchhiker's Guide to the Galaxy* (mad philosophical science fiction, its sequels are funny too. I'd say it was the closest thing to a surefire laugh if that wasn't tempting fate)
2 Roald Dahl - *Revolting Rhymes and Dirty Beasts* (poems)
3 TS Eliot - *Old Possum's Book of Practical Cats* (poems)
4 The poems of Ogden Nash (Google him)
5 Evelyn Waugh - *Scoop!*
6 Stella Gibbons - *Cold Comfort Farm*
7 PG Wodehouse (pronounced 'Woodhouse') - *The Code of the Woosters* (there are loads more Jeeves and Wooster books, and some great other Wodehouse ones too)
8 George and Weedon Grossmith - *The Diary of a Nobody*
9 Oscar Wilde - *The Importance of Being Earnest* (a play, maybe the funniest one in English)
10 Tom Stoppard - *Rosencrantz and Guildenstern Are Dead* (also a play, also funny)

11 Jerome K Jerome - *Three Men in a Boat*
12 Sue Townsend - *The Secret Diary of Adrian Mole Aged 13 ¾*
13 Joseph Heller - *Catch 22*
14 Philip Roth - *Portnoy's Complaint*
15 Nina Stibbe - *Love, Nina*

Comics and graphic novels

1 Charles Schultz - *Peanuts* (five decades of daily, three-panel comic strips)
2 Bill Watterson - *Calvin and Hobbes* (just the one decade, so only around 3000 strips)
3 The New Yorker cartoons (a century of single panel jokes by thousands of artists)
4 Marjane Satrapi - *Persepolis*
5 Alan Moore and Eddie Campbell - *From Hell*
6 Alan Moore and Dave Gibbons - *Watchmen*
7 Art Spiegelman - *Maus*
8 Alejandro Jodorowsky and Jean Giraud - *The Incal*
9 Alison Bechdel - *Fun Home* and *Are You My Mother*?
10 Seth - *It's a Good Life, If You Don't Weaken*
11 Scott McCloud - *Understanding Comics* (brilliant, especially if you want to write comics/graphic novels yourself)

Non-fiction (generally not funny)

I don't know what you're interested in – only what I am – but here are some books that have changed the way I see the world.

They're pretty varied. I will say I don't regret reading the two philosophy books in this list, a subject I was completely ignorant of until I started writing this book.

Beyond that, ask people you respect for suggestions, with some general ideas about topics you're interested in. But, of course, you can't know whether you'd be interested in a subject if you don't know it exists. So cast your net widely and sometimes blindly.

1. Malcolm Gladwell - anything
2. Nigel Warburton - *A Little History of Philosophy* (short, fun introductions to 40 major Western thinkers of the past 2500 years; very dip-in-and-outable)
3. Simon Flynn - *The Science Magpie* (also very dippable)
4. Andre Comte-Sponville - *The Little Book of Philosophy*
5. *The GCHQ Puzzle Book*
6. EH Gombrich - *A Little History of the World* (again, dip in and out)
7. Yuval Noah Harari - *Sapiens* (a 200,000 year history of our species)
8. Yuval Noah Harari - *Homo Deus* (a look at its future)
9. Simon Schama - *A History of England* (there's also a good TV version)
10. Stephen Hawking - *A Brief History of Time*
11. Simon Singh - *Fermat's Last Theorem*
12. Oliver Sacks - *The Man Who Mistook His Wife for a Hat*

13 Daniel Kahneman - *Thinking Fast and Slow* (start anywhere and snack on five-ten pages at a time)

14 Richard Dawkins - *The Selfish Gene*

15 Henry Kissinger - *World Order* (born German Jewish in 1923, then a child refugee from Nazi Germany to America, then a Gestapo-hunting GI in 1944, Kissinger has spent more than half of his long and extraordinary life influencing American foreign policy, under several presidents, including the current one. To many on the Left Wing, he's a cynical warmonger and an enemy of democracy (Chile 1973 is just one of many examples). But his views on history are brilliant)

16 Niccolo Machiavelli - *The Prince*

17 Thomas Hobbes - *Leviathan*

18 Sun Tzu - *The Art of War* (these last three are all in the same vein as Kissinger's book – they're about the use of political and military power – but older and shorter)

Non-fiction websites

1 *London Review of Books* and the *New York Review of Books* (around half the content is free, and the archives stretch back decades, so you can always find something interesting. Serious books of all kinds are reviewed by subject experts who summarise their arguments then respond with their own ones, so reading 3000 words feels like getting two whole books)

2 *XKCD* (somewhat similar, except it's all in single-panel cartoons – the one on Judgment Day is good)

3 *Brain Pickings* (extraordinary website by Maria Popova, who has spent a decade filleting some of the greatest fiction and non-fiction books of the past 200 years)

4 *Wait But Why* (thoughtful enquiries into life by a scientifically-minded guy on questions like how to choose a life partner or why procastinators procastinate, and on subjects like Artificial Intelligence or the Fermi Paradox)

5 *The Sceptical Doctor* (comprehensive site, run by a fan, collating columns by my favourite right-wing writer Theodore Dalrymple, a retired prison psychiatrist – and unlike most right-wing stuff it's all free, no paywall)

6 *Unherd* (the only place I know that hosts top-notch political writing from both right and left wings)

7 *Project Syndicate* (essays by political and economic heavyweights about how to fix the world)

8 *So You Want To Study Engineering* (interesting and hard maths and logic problems with tips and walk-throughs that keep me interested, despite my inability to do most of the questions. Created by a Cambridge professor who uses these questions in undergraduate interviews – so, hard)

9 Oxford and Cambridge interview questions (both universities have started releasing questions across many subjects and, crucially, telling you how to answer them. A really good

snapshot of what the tutorial teaching system there is like, for anyone who's curious, e.g. 'Ladybirds are red. So are strawberries. Why?')

10 Eton College Kings Scholarship past papers (especially the general papers, which always have an interesting chunk of philosophy. You might be surprised at the intellectual standard some 13-year-olds are at. Eton publishes at least a decade's worth of its past papers, and these papers are my favourite teaching aid, bar none. Sample question: 'Wars are always won by the side with the most advanced technology. Discuss'. Westminster publishes the past three years of its similar Challenge scholarship exam)

11 All Souls College exam past papers (this postgraduate Oxford college sets perhaps the world's hardest exam to undergraduates who got the top first class degrees in every subject. Sample question: 'Does it matter what a judge had for breakfast?')

12 *Wikipedia* (extraordinary public resource without which this book would have been much harder to write, and one of the unambiguously great things to come out of the Information Revolution. Many of the websites on this list rely on public donations to keep going, and this is one I donate to)

13 *The Electric Typewriter* (a broad range of essays by celebrated writers and journalists)

Poems

I've given no poet names because I want you to Google them. I've mostly, and deliberately, chosen very short poems, many half a page long.[6] If you want to stick them on a wall in your garret like I did,[7] or if you're short-sighted like I am, you'll want them to be in as large text as possible. Honestly, you might read one or none of the books on these lists. Don't worry. Most people are busy.

But a poem is short. Lyric poems, that is, like these ones – rather than epic poems which are novel-length and tell a story – describe a moment, and mostly take 1-30 seconds to read. Another 30 to re-read, if something in it grabs you and you can't work out why. Maybe one or two bits of it will stick somewhere in your head and occur to you in an idle moment weeks or months later. Or, if you like one, if it seems to you to express something useful or true, then spend five or 15 minutes learning it by heart so it's available to you forever and everywhere.

I think that's what poetry is for. To clarify our thoughts with words we couldn't have found on our own.

---

[6] I think the shortest one on this list is 'This is just to say', which I recommend reading alongside the work of R. Mutt (do a Google image search).

[7] Or anywhere, but not in your car. 'Wordsworth was almost the price of me once,' Philip Larkin told an interviewer, because 'Daffodils' once came on Radio 4 while he was driving down a motorway and he teared up; nearly swerving into the central partition.

Franz Kakfa[8] said that 'A book must be the axe for the frozen sea within us'. I think a poem's a similar tool but smaller. Maybe more an ice-pick for chiselling lumps to chill your drinks than a hatchet for freeing frozen ships – but useful nonetheless.

1. Shall I compare thee to a summer's day?
2. The Sun Rising
3. The Garden
4. Ask not for whom the bell tolls (not a poem, actually a sermon, but it's short, and it was written by a poet)
5. Elegy Written in a Country Churchyard
6. The Tyger
7. Jerusalem
8. Ozymandias
9. I Wandered Lonely as a Cloud
10. Ulysses
11. Crossing the Bar
12. My Last Duchess
13. The Windhover
14. Afterwards
15. Dover Beach
16. 'Hope' is the Thing with Feathers
17. Because I could not stop for Death

[8] Kafka is famous for *The Trial* and *The Metamorphosis*, though my favourite is his short story 'The Great Wall of China'.

18 If

19 Shibboleth

20 All My Sad Captains

21 Prime Numbers

22 The Lake Isle of Innisfree

23 The Waste Land

24 Do not go gentle into that good night

25 Musée des Beaux Arts

26 Atlantis

27 Days

28 The Mower

29 The Road Less Travelled

30 The Emperor of Ice Cream

31 This is just to say

32 A Lullaby

33 The Fish

34 The Gettysburg Address (not a poem but a speech, delivered in 1863 to the Union army before the Battle of Gettysburg in the American Civil War, in which the anti-slavery North – the Union – would defeat the pro-slavery South – the Confederacy – and set America on its course to become the greatest nation in the world)

Part two: representation and the canon

If you're female you've probably noticed there aren't many women on this reading list. If you're not white you've probably noticed the list is pretty white. And if you're not white and a woman you've probably noticed both these things. But if you're white and male, like me, it's possible you haven't noticed any of this, because in-group people like us tend not to notice things like that, even though they benefit us in all sorts of ways. We just assume it's the natural order of things. Well, it's not.

In this list there are fewer books written by women, or by people who aren't white, or by people who aren't from the upper- or upper-middle classes. That's partly because, for most of the 1200-year history of English literature, anyone other than upper-middle-class white males weren't encouraged to write books. For most of that time, many people weren't even taught to read. And even then they were excluded from writing books, and even if they wrote books, the people who owned the printing presses that made books, who were usually upper- and upper-middle-class white men, didn't usually publish books by people who weren't like them.

Dead White Males

For all the reasons listed above, Dead White Males are heavily overrepresented in almost every field of human endeavour. The white part is probably there because it was a few white Europeans 500 years ago who conquered and settled the New World of North and South America, and exploited those continents' natural resources and people, whose wealth gave them the leisure time to study the world more widely. The male part goes back much further to the Agricultural Revolution 10,000 years ago, when a few men seized the benefits of lots of farmers for themselves, and compensated the remaining men by giving them power over women. Feminists call this system the Patriarchy.

This isn't a reading list

This isn't a reading list. I'm not *telling you* to read these books. This list is certainly not representative of the world of books in 2019, or even in 1988, when I was ten and started reading 'grown-up' books for myself. But it is somewhat representative of the *literary* world of 1988, and therefore of 2019, because *that* world – the sphere of books that are considered to be *literature* – changes quite slowly. John Updike, an American who wrote 29 novels, complained about his 'ponderously growing oeuvre, dragging behind me like an ever-heavier tail'. Well, literature in English has been going for well over 1000 years, which is a long tail by any measure (though Greek and Italian/Latin literature have longer histories, and Indian and Chinese longer ones still).

To modern eyes it was very unfair back then, and, more

to the point, it still is. You're reading a book written by an apparently upper-middle-class white man. It was hard for me to get this book published: I wrote to 40 literary agents to find one willing to represent me. I know, *boo-hoo*. But it would have been harder still if I weren't from this privileged class, or in-group.

There are two kinds of aristocracy in history. There's the traditional aristocracy of power/land/money, which is largely a closed shop, because it's hereditary, and because power/land/money are all finite things (though if you look up 'fiat currency' you may be surprised), and these finite things have always been – and will always be – shared unequally.

And then there's the second kind of aristocracy, the aristocracy of the mind, which was until recently also a somewhat closed shop – because libraries, and people who can read, have always been in short supply. Until 1440 and Gutenberg's press, the only books the few literate people (monks) had to read were the ones copied out by hand by other literate people (other monks).

So these two aristocracies have throughout history looked quite similar. Only the first kind of aristocracy has had the leisure time – and access to libraries and universities and publishers – that enabled a (very) few of them to become the second kind of aristocracy, the aristocracy of the mind.

Over the past two centuries, mass literacy, public libraries, publicly-funded education and the internet have slowly opened up the world of the mind, to vastly more people than ever before had access to the best of human thought. It remains to be seen what we'll do with it.

Standpoint theory versus 'you are unimaginable'

In 1807, the German philosopher Georg Wilhelm Friedrich Hegel came up with standpoint theory. It states that the viewpoints (or standpoints) of a master and a slave must be different, because of their very different experiences of life. In 1983, Nancy Hartsock focused this idea on feminist theory (female/male relations) rather than Hegel/Marxist class theory (master/slave relations). And it has been also applied to the standpoints of non-white people and LGBT people, and other out-groups.

Sandra Harding's related theory of strong objectivity states that it isn't possible for anyone's standpoint to be truly neutral however hard they try – she calls this weak objectivity. Objective in common English means 'universally true'; whereas subjective means 'personally true' – something may be true from your perspective, but it won't be true for everyone, because everyone else has very different experiences of life, and those experiences affect what is true for them.

'This is my truth, tell me yours', as the Labour politician Aneurin Bevan said (he was the creator of the NHS), suggesting that 'truth' is a subjective, personal thing, but also that, when many people's truths are combined into one, that collective 'truth' can become objective, and universally true. Strong objectivity goes further than this by saying that it's the perspectives of out-groups that need to be combined to make this universal and objective truth.

This is not just because the perspectives of these groups have traditionally been excluded and ignored by the in-groups who are in charge of deciding what the truth is. It's also because these out-groups have special knowledge of how society works – of how racism, sexism, homophobia and class prejudice, in their many forms, both obvious and subtle, all work – because only they have had personal experience of them.

In the 1996 film *Jerry Maguire*, a sports agent (Jerry, who is dating a single mother) asks his client (Rod, an American footballer) for advice on his love life:

> Jerry: What do you know about dating a single mother?
> Rod: Oh I know plenty. I was raised by a single mother.
> Jerry: Tell me, because it's been a month, and she's about to take another job in San Diego.
> Rod: First, single mothers don't 'date'. They have been to the circus, you know what I'm saying? They have been to the puppet show and they have seen the strings.

Rod isn't a single mother himself – he's married, and a multi-millionaire – but what he says about single mothers supports the theory of strong objectivity. Single mothers have already experienced the breakdown of a marriage and a family, so their perspective on romantic love – on 'dating' – is deeper than the perspective of someone who's never been married and had children, and then had that marriage collapse. They have more at stake when they're dating, because they have the security and happiness of their child to consider, as well as their own, and they have first-hand experience of what it's like when romantic love breaks down: single mothers, as Rod says, 'have seen the strings'.

Imaginative empathy

Anyone who writes a story that isn't strictly autobiographical has to imagine another person's perspective – their narrator's for one thing. And that narrator – let alone any of their characters – is rarely exactly the same person as the one writing the book. If the novelist has invented any of the story – and they must have if it's a novel – then the characters in it must have experienced life differently from the person writing their story, and their perspective must therefore be different from the novelist's.

According to standpoint theory, a novelist can't possibly know what it's like to be someone else. So what do they do?

Well, they do research – they ask people, and they read – about what that someone's else's life might be like. And then, using imaginative empathy – given what that someone else's life is like on the outside, what is it like on the inside? What is it like to be that someone else? – they make it up.

And anyone who reads a story is using the same skill, of imaginative empathy, which is how they put themselves in the shoes of the main character. Reading is just as much of a creative and imaginative act as writing, because a story isn't a pill you take to feel certain feelings and think certain thoughts as prescribed by the author – it's one human being engaging with another human being in order to imagine the world of a third one.

Quarantine (Italian for '40 days') is a novel by Jim Crace that imagines the thoughts of Jesus Christ as he spends 40 days and nights alone in the desert. Now, Jim Crace had probably read the New Testament,[9] which describes this period in Jesus's life, and he might have spent time alone in a desert himself to research what it felt like, or at least read about deserts. But he, a 20th-century Englishman, couldn't *know* what it was like for Jesus, a half-man, half-god who lived two thousand years ago. He made it up.

The problem with standpoint theory and stories

Standpoint theory and strong objectivity are ideas from philosophy, which tries to explain life. And stories are not a part

[9] Specifically the four Gospels, which were written by four of Jesus's disciples – and not by Jesus – so, again, they weren't there in the desert either.

of life, although they try to imagine something like it. Stories are an art form, and art is distinct from life: the same rules do not apply. Storytellers are free to imagine lives quite unlike their own.

Lionel Shriver, the author of *We Need to Talk About Kevin* (whose narrator is Armenian-American, despite Shriver being German-American), has defended this freedom, for herself and other authors:

> I find it an enormous relief to escape the confines of my own head. Even if novels and short stories only do so by creating an illusion, fiction helps to fell the exasperating barriers between us, and for a short while allows us to behold the astonishing reality of other people.

This freedom, for writers and readers alike, is a thing that connects people who are on the face of it unlike each other, because our thoughts, feelings and perspectives may be strongly affected by the lives we have lived and our ethnicity, gender, sexuality and class – but they're not unique to us, or the different in- or out-groups that we belong to. One of the great pleasures of reading as widely as you can is realising that someone completely different to you in all the ways that matter in the real world, who may have lived on the other side of the world 1000 years ago, has had the exact same thought that you once had.

The novel is perhaps, along with the essay, the most interior of all art forms. In films and television we see the characters behave in the world, and we hear them talk, and we infer from these two things what sort of people they are. But we are greatly influenced by what they look and sound like while they are doing these things. And we never hear them think.

In novels, we do. Even if the faces, bodies and voices of a novel's characters are described for us, those descriptions are coming from inside another human mind. And even if our narrators are unreliable, as they often are in 20th-century novels, we're still up close to – or even inside – another human mind, like ours in some ways, different in others, thinking their thoughts and feeling their feelings in a way that dissolves barriers of time and place and gender and race and class.

Terence, a North African[10] slave who was freed and became one of Ancient Rome's greatest playwrights, wrote that: 'I am human, and I think nothing human is alien to me'.

The universalising effect of the novel, the way it puts you inside the like mind of another human being who could look quite unlike you on the outside, is the same for those who

[10] Professor Mary Beard has pointed out that, while the Roman Empire was multi-ethnic, as Europe is today, ethnicity didn't matter nearly as much as the division between slave and citizen, or civilised (i.e. being part of the Empire) and barbarian. The website eidolon.pub has lots of great essays about the ancient world that connects it to the modern one.

read them and those who write them – who, if they're any good, also read widely.

Does the English-Japanese novelist Kazuo Ishiguro only read books by English-Japanese writers? No; he wrote *The Sleeping Giant*, a story in which the mythical Arthurian (white, male, medieval) knight Sir Gawain plays a major part. Ishiguro has presumably read the Arthurian myths, even though they contain no Anglo-Japanese characters. He also wrote *The Remains of the Day*, about a white working-class butler who worked for a Nazi-sympathising aristocrat in England in the 1930s.

Does Zadie Smith stick to reading books written by mixed-race British writers? No; she wrote *On Beauty*, which is essentially a modern retelling of a 100-year-old novel by EM Forster, *Howard's End*, written by a gay, white, upper-middle-class man, who wasn't openly gay in the 1920s because it was illegal then (homosexuality – another 'out-group' – was legalised in 1967 in the UK). Two very different people, if you were to just look at them, who nevertheless managed to tell the same story, which I'd suggest tells us that what makes a story, and what makes a writer, doesn't totally depend on their gender, or their class, or their ethnicity.

Imagining what other people's lives are like, by writing them, and by reading them, is one of the things that makes civilisation possible.

As the British-Pakistani novelist Kamila Shamsie[11] puts it:

> 'You – other – are unimaginable' is a far more problematic attitude than 'You are imaginable'.

Science versus literature

The physicist Stephen Hawking in his book *A Brief History of Time* tells a funny story about a famous astronomer confronted after his lecture by an elderly lady who disputes his version of the universe. She insists instead that the world sits on the back of a giant tortoise.

'Ah,' says the astronomer, 'but what does the tortoise sit on?'

The lady replies, 'You're very clever, young man, very clever. But it's turtles all the way down'.

Literature isn't like science. Living writers are influenced by dead ones, deeply so, but one work of art doesn't replace another, however great or truthful it may be. Works of literature just sit there, read or unread, loved or unloved, their reputations growing or decaying over the centuries. In the 350 years since Milton published *Paradise Lost*, no one has written a long poem in English as good as it, in my view. It's

[11] I haven't read her 2017 novel *Home Fire*, but I have seen it on the shelves of a couple of friends who are better read than me.

an open question whether anyone managed it before him, though Chaucer's *The Canterbury Tales* and the anonymous *Beowulf* poet have strong claims. But since 1667, no one. William Wordsworth wrote *The Prelude* which was part of a longer poem *The Recluse* which he never finished. William Blake wrote a couple of long poems, one of which was called Milton, neither of which are much read these days. Byron's *Don Juan* is brilliant and sexy and funny as hell, but not sublime – 'possessing an almost Godlike vision and greatness' – like *Paradise Lost.*

The thing about literature, though – it is turtles all the way down. A great work of art doesn't replace another, or improve on it. One way of thinking about this is to look at the sequels to great movies. I'm not talking about Marvel or DC superhero movies, or *Harry Potter* ones, many of which are good, but none of which are great (if you disagree with this judgement, I'm afraid you just haven't seen enough movies). Sequels to great movies are almost never as good as the original. The *Godfather II* and *Terminator II* are maybe as good as their originals. Krzysztof Kieślowski's *Three Colours* trilogy to my mind actually improves over the course of its three films. But these are very rare exceptions.

Science is iterative; art isn't.

On bastards

As Mark Antony said in the funeral speech for his friend Julius Caesar in Shakespeare's play *Julius Caesar*:

> The evil that men do lives after them;
> The good is oft interred with their bones.

But this isn't true of great writers, whose works ('The good') survives on the printed page. We also, however, increasingly hear about the evil that these writers – and the real bastards of literature are almost always men – did in their lives. One or two great writers have killed another human being in peacetime – and rather more if you include killing in wars – but I'm going to focus on a few less extreme examples of 'evil' in some of my favourite writers. Writing and researching this book has occasionally been disillusioning as I've come across unpleasant details of the lives of some of my literary heroes. But I haven't removed any of their books from my lists, for reasons I'll explain shortly.

Roald Dahl, before he became one of the great children's writers of the 20th century, fought as a fighter pilot against the Nazis in the Second World War. In his (adult) short story 'A Piece of Cake', he describes shooting down an enemy plane over the Mediterranean Sea, where the German pilot certainly drowned – if he hadn't already been killed by Dahl's guns or burned alive. He shot down several more enemy planes during the war. So Roald Dahl certainly killed people, even though it was in a just war against a hateful genocidal ideology.

But here's where it gets tricky. Despite fighting against the Nazis, it turns out Dahl held some unpleasantly anti-Semitic views himself. 'There is a trait in the Jewish character that does provoke animosity,' he said in 1983, '... even a stinker like Hitler didn't just pick on them for no reason.' The context of this comment was Israel's bombing of Palestine, which killed thousands, but that context isn't strictly relevant. What is relevant is that Dahl believed there was such a thing as a 'Jewish character' – that basically 'they're all the same' – which is one of the hallmarks of a racist. And though he condemns Hitler, he also gets halfway to saying that the Jews brought the Holocaust on themselves, that 'Hitler didn't just pick on them for no reason'.

These comments are apparently the reason why the Royal Mail recently decided against publicly commemorating the 100th anniversary of Roald Dahl's birth on its stamps, stating that he was '...associated with anti-Semitism and not regarded as an author of the highest reputation'. This is quite right.

What is also right, though, is that his marvellous books continue to be read and enjoyed by millions of children around the world. The books – which I've never heard being described as anti-Semitic – and the man – especially now that the man is dead – are separate things and should be treated separately.

The poet Philip Larkin, in private letters to friends that were published after his death, expressed racist and sexist views that – even though they're absent from his poetry to my mind – have spoiled him for some readers. That's fair enough. His father was a Nazi sympathiser, which goes some way to explaining his racism. Larkin described himself as 'one of those old-type natural fouled-up guys'. A few critics have gone so far as to call him a 'misogynist' – a man who hates women – which seems too strong; misogynist is a word which some people use when what they really mean is 'sexist'. He never married but had several long relationships with women, whom he seems to have treated well; or at least, to have not treated badly.

In 'Talking in Bed', Larkin ponders the difference between the two, and the difficulty of doing either:

At this unique distance from isolation
It becomes still more difficult to find
Words at once true and kind,
Or not untrue and not unkind.

His poetry recognises how hard love can be for some people – for everyone, sometimes – which I think is why it is still so widely read.

In 'Wild Oats' Larkin concludes:

That I was too selfish, withdrawn,
And easily bored to love.

For him, love is more easily described by its absence, more readily compared to the 'voice' (actually clarinet) of an African American jazz musician he revered, as in 'For Sidney Bechet':

On me your voice falls as they say love should,
Like an enormous yes.

Despite being an atheist with an unquenchable fear of death (his poems' greatest preoccupation), Larkin nevertheless gravitated to churches. In 'An Arundel Tomb' he deliberately misunderstands the clasped gloves of a medieval earl and countess, rendered in stone on their mausoleum, sentimentally believing the reclining statues' hand-holding

...to prove
Our almost-instinct almost true:
What will survive of us is love.

If it sounds like I'm just regurgitating a 20-year-old A-Level essay, you'd be right. But that's the point. The fact that I can do that – I don't think I've taught any of these four poems in the past two decades – shows what these words still mean to me. They're words that have informed and influenced the way I think about my own life, which is exactly what literature is for.

And, by the way, if it sounds like I've given up on defending the man and am now defending the poetry, you're also right – not that Larkin's poetry needs much help from me. I honestly don't know if I would have liked the man had I met him – certainly his biographer, the poet Andrew Motion, refused to listen to the racist and sexist views he offered freely in private. And the argument/excuse mooted by some that he was a product of his times – he was roughly a contemporary of Roald Dahl – only goes so far. Larkin would have been in his 90s today (he died in 1985), and I've known men of his generation who didn't hold those hateful views.

Chinua Achebe, the Nigerian author of one of the books on my list – *Things Fall Apart* – had a lot to say about what he believed was the racist attitude of another book I include: *Heart of Darkness*, by Joseph Conrad. Achebe argues that Conrad's book, most of which is set on a journey up the River Congo, but whose main characters are all white, uses Africans as a mere backdrop to the story, and denies their humanity. As he says: 'My humanity is not to be debated, nor is it to be used simply to illustrate European problems'.

Chinua Achebe's objection to Joseph Conrad was not

that he was racist, but that his book was. And, as he witheringly says, great books are more than just 'good sentences'. For people who take literature seriously, great books show us a moral framework about what life is like, and how it should be lived. For Conrad to write an African novel that pays such scant regard to Africans is a serious failure. His narrator Marlow is the worst kind of tourist, looking inward when he should be looking out. But perhaps the novel's flaw is the same flaw of most of the Europeans who took part in the 19th century's 'Race for Africa'. Whether they were racing to grab what they saw as virgin territory, or to convert Africans to Christianity and thereby save their savage souls, very few of them paid any mind to the wishes of the natives on whose continent they were trespassing.

That said, *Heart of Darkness* is still a great novel, worth reading despite, or perhaps because of, this flaw. There aren't that many great books, and we shouldn't reject such books lightly, whatever the reputations of their writers. And, if necessary, we should try to salvage worthwhile and moral books from the wreckage of their authors' lives. As Mozart says to Emperor Joseph II in Peter Shaffer's play *Amadeus*:

> Forgive me, Majesty. I am a vulgar man! But I assure you, my music is not.

What are stories for?

Luckily, better minds than mine have pondered this question, so I'm just going to lay out some of my favourite definitions of what stories – or literature, which just means old stories that are still worth reading – are actually for:

> Stories are equipment for living.
> *Kenneth Burke*

> What oft was thought, but ne'er so well expressed.
> *Alexander Pope* (who was actually trying to define 'wit')

> Literature is news that stays news.
> *Ezra Pound*

> Our literature is a substitute for religion, and so is our religion.
> *TS Eliot*

TS Eliot also said that 'Meaning is the juicy bone a burglar throws your dog as he goes about the business of robbing your house'. Which is to say that great writing operates on many levels, and if we think we've understood everything about one of these great books – I'm talking mostly about the really old ones here – then we're probably mistaken.

The Seven Basic Plots, by Christopher Booker, is the book to read if you want to understand how stories work. The most thrilling part is the opening chapter, in which the writer lays out exactly how the first half of *Beowulf*, where Beowulf battles the monster Grendel who is devouring innocent people, is at heart the same story as Steven Spielberg's *Jaws* 1200 years later, in which the hero battles a giant shark which is devouring innocent people. And *The Tale of Peter Rabbit* by Beatrix Potter is the same basic story: Peter Rabbit escapes his own monster, Mr McGregor, though Peter doesn't also kill him – it's a children's story. Here are what Christopher Booker thinks are the seven kinds of stories:

1. Escaping the Monster (*Beowulf*, *Jaws*, all horror movies)
2. Rags to Riches (Cinderella)
3. The Quest (Jason and the Golden Fleece)
4. Voyage and Return (*Alice in Wonderland*)
5. Comedy (*Much Ado About Nothing, Some Like It Hot*)
6. Tragedy (*Hamlet*, *Oedipus Rex*)
7. Rebirth (*A Christmas Carol*)

Ultimately, you read a story because you think it will entertain you, and because you hope it will tell you something about life: another person's, of course, but through it your own. People who can do both these things are rare, but they're also everywhere.

WH Auden put it this way:

> A poet's hope: to be, like some valley cheese, local, but prized elsewhere.

The dead

There are seven billion people alive now, roughly, and 107 billion who have lived and are now dead. We, the living, are in the minority. And it's this majority, the dead, who outnumber us 15-1, and whose under-representation in most people's reading habits I want to talk about.

Reading books by dead people is absolutely, *numero uno*, without any doubt, by a million miles the very best thing you can do to guarantee success in your education, and, I'd argue, your life. Why?

Well, here's dead poet WH Auden's answer to that question:

> Some books are undeservedly forgotten; none are undeservedly remembered.

If you read a lot of dead authors, you're reading the best books of their time, because none of the bad books of their time are still in print. You're also – and this isn't a small thing – reading the best books of all time. A classic is defined as a book that has never finished saying what it has to say; it's news that stays news. The *Harry Potter* books have outsold every book ever written except for the Bible, but the real test is whether they'll still be read in 100 years. Actually, the real test is whether, like the Bible, they'll be read in 2000 years.

Also, if you want to make a thorough study of English literature, then you'll have to spend as much time reading books written 1200 years ago as those written 100 years ago. Shakespeare only died about 400 years ago, and is considered an 'Early Modern' writer. The 400 years before his birth are called 'Middle English' (Chaucer and the unnamed 'Gawain poet' are the big stars of this era), and the 400 years before that are known as 'Old English' or 'Anglo-Saxon', a period which mostly predates the Norman Conquest (named after the Normans – who turned up in 1066 speaking French, completely confusing the Old High German-speaking Anglo-Saxons). The also-nameless Beowulf poet is the big star of the Old English era, and if you read Seamus Heaney's modern translation of *Beowulf* you'll get a really good sense of perhaps the greatest poem in English (along with Chaucer's *The Canterbury Tales* and Milton's *Paradise Lost*), and one which inspired large parts of JRR Tolkien's *The Lord of the Rings*.

'Count no man lucky until he is dead' said the Athenian wise man Solon to the legendarily wealthy Lydian king Croesus, who was bragging to Solon about his riches. Croesus was later murdered by his son who ruled in his place, which kind of proved Solon's point.

Great books are the same – they're only great because they've been considered great for many years after their author has died. And the greatest of these great books are the ones that inspired other great books. The Greek poet Homer's *Odyssey* (eighth century BCE, or BC) inspired the Roman poet Virgil's *Aeneid*, (first century CE, or AD) which – along with The Bible – inspired the Italian Dante's *Divine Comedy* (14th century CE), which inspired Milton's 17th-century *Paradise Lost*.

This kind of greatness, the greatness of Homer, belongs only to books which have survived for centuries – millennia, even – and survived because they had something to say to each succeeding generation, who preserved them because of it.

Primary and secondary epic

In Homer's case – in the case of his two epic poems *The Iliad* (about the Trojan War) and *The Odyssey* (about Odysseus's long journey home afterwards) – his work's survival is even more remarkable, because Homer was writing at a time when hardly anyone in Europe could read or write. Actually, the poet we call 'Homer' is not one but many poets. The events of Homer's two poems – the war between the Greeks and Troy, and one Greek hero's journey home to Ithaca – all took place 400 years before Homer wrote them down. And, while these stories were preserved by poets in those 400 years, they were not written down, preserved with pen and ink. No. All these other poets, the ones we call 'Homer', had to memorise the words of these two poems – hundreds of thousands of them, over tens of thousands of lines – in order to pass them on to the next generation. The poet we call Homer was simply the first of these dozens, perhaps hundreds of poets, to write these poems down.

Here is the definition of primary epic, as given by JRR Tolkien, who knew a thing or two about epics (he wrote *The Lord of the Rings*, which could probably be counted as a secondary epic, even though it's written in prose, rather than poetry like most epics). So. Primary epics are long poems that come from an oral tradition. They were told, by many poets – I'm going to use the word bards here to mean old-time poets from this oral tradition – and were only written down after several generations of bards had performed and refined them.

Tolkien's favourite poem *Beowulf*, which he freely borrowed from in *The Hobbit*, is another example of primary epic, because the story of its sixth-century Scandinavian hero Beowulf had been passed down orally, by generations of illiterate bards, before an anonymous English monk actually wrote it down in the tenth century, 400 years later.

Secondary epics are long poems – like primary epics they're often about the founding of a nation, or a war – but they have just one author, who came up with the whole thing himself. Virgil, Dante and Milton are all authors of secondary epics, because – although they were all hugely influenced by Homer's two great primary epics – they were literate, and they invented and wrote down their epic poems all on their own, without the help of a centuries-old oral tradition.

I suppose you could compare primary epics to old recipes that have been passed down in families for generations, and don't really have a single creator. Whereas secondary epics are more like the cronut (invented by Dominique Ansel in New York in 2013), or ciabatta (invented by Arnaldo Cavallari in Verona in 1982).

Anyway, enough of these food analogies. They're making me hungry.

Medieval tales and ancient epics

Going even deeper into the real heavy stuff, you might come across:

1. *Grimm's Fairy Tales* (read in any order; there's a good translation by Philip Pullman, whose own books are worth a look)
2. Norse Myths (translations by AS Byatt and Neil Gaiman, both of whose own books are also excellent)
3. *Aesop's Fables* (dip in)
4. *Beowulf* (there's a great translation by Seamus Heaney, whose own poems etc etc)
5. *The Arabian Nights*, aka *The 1001 Nights* (read, from start to

finish, about Sheherazade, who tells all the stories – or skip to her greatest hits: Ali Baba, Sinbad, Aladdin)

6 Ovid's *Metamorphoses* (the Penguin translation is good, as is the Oxford edition, which is translated into poetry – the Latin original is a poem – but either way skip book one, or better still look in the index of characters and just read the bits about the characters you've heard of; there'll be lots, because it's a compendium of all the big Greek Myths; and if you find it too heavy try Stephen Fry's new book *Mythos*)

7 Apart from Ovid (my favourite) the other big Roman poets are Virgil (his epic *The Aeneid* is Rome's official founding myth), Horace (shorter odes about wine and keeping things simple), Catullus (short poems of heartbreak and shorter ones obscenely abusing his enemies) and Martial (two-line epigrams that seem to comprehend life in its entirety – seriously, Google his best lines: until recently I thought it was Theresa May or David Goodhart who said that 'A man who lives everywhere lives nowhere')

8 If you've read all these you could have a go at the greatest poem in English, *Paradise Lost.* Try John Carey's 'Essential' version, he's shortened it by two thirds – I promise you, you'll thank me. If you somehow get through that, you'll like William Blake and James Hogg (both similarly potty), and if you still want more try Homer, Dante, and William Wordsworth's *The Prelude*

9 Thomas Malory's *Morte d'Arthur* – The Death of Arthur – is

the authoritative English version of the Arthur myth, but it's 500 years old and a tough read, so skip to the last two or three parts. *The Once and Future King*, by TH White, is the best modern retelling

10 Early Shakespeare if you want blood (*Titus Andronicus*) or japes, and late Shakespeare if you want both at the same time (*A Winter's Tale*), but Middle Shakespeare is where the five great tragedies are: *Hamlet* (a great read, and my favourite), *King Lear*, *Macbeth*, *Othello*, *Romeo and Juliet*

11 History: *The Decline and Fall of the Roman Empire* by Edward Gibbon; the actual Romans Livy (authoritative), Tacitus (sly, ironic), Suetonius (scandalous) and (Shakespeare's favourite) Plutarch; and the Greeks Thucydides and Xenophon and Herodotus (sometimes called the father of history, though he's really its dodgy uncle: lots of mad stuff about ants as big as dogs and crocodiles wearing jewellery that he may have just made up)

12 Anything by Aristotle (*Poetics*, *Rhetoric*, or *Nicomachean Ethics*), or anything by his teacher Plato (especially *The Republic*), though *his* teacher, Socrates, couldn't write, or wouldn't, so all we have of his teachings is what Plato wrote down about him

13 The Bible (which contains the Old (Jewish) and New (Christian) Testaments, ideally in the King James version). *Bible Stories*, also known as the Old Testament, are a good (easier) retelling by Leon Kossoff

14 The Qu'ran, the Tao Te Ching (there's a translation by Ursula le Guin), the Zhuangzi, the Bhagavad Gita, The Tibetan Book of the Dead, the sayings of Buddha and Confucius, and any other major world religion's foundational texts you can get your hands on.

For many of these books, which aren't really 'books' in the strictest sense of having been made up and written down by a single author, you should go for a fairly modern version, let's say one written in the last 50 years, and ideally – I can't stress this enough – in an edition that has lots of pictures. The main point about these stories is that they all existed long before they were written down, so there's no definitive version you should read them in. In fact, it's really up to you how you want to. Maybe read two versions and think about why they're different.

My route, aged eight, into the long-lost world of these stories was via a book called *Greek Myths* which, in my edition, had terrifying full-colour, full-page pictures of Polyphemus, the one-eyed giant (Cyclops) just blinded by Odysseus, groping vengefully under his (also giant) sheep because he suspected, rightly, that Odysseus and his men were hiding under them in order to escape his cave, where he meant to murder and eat them. Pretty gripping stuff when you're eight. Extensive Googling has failed to turn up this book: it's probably out of print and was published at least 30 years ago.

Sir Gawain and the Loathly Damsel, memorably illustrated and retold for children by Joanna Troughton, was another book I read and re-read dozens of times when I was very young; years later I was amazed to find that the same story had been told six centuries earlier by Chaucer as 'The Wife of Bath's Tale' in *The Canterbury Tales*, and in the Gawain poet's Arthurian masterpiece *Sir Gawain and the Green Knight*. Great stories stay with you for decades, and they stick around for centuries, as long as people keep reading them.

We're lucky to live in an age of great storytellers, but never forget that every age before us – even those before writing – was similarly blessed. And I bet if you asked JK Rowling or Philip Pullman or Neil Gaiman where you should start reading, or if you could commune with the dead and ask JRR Tolkien or TH White or CS Lewis[12] the same question – well, I bet they would tell you to leave off reading their books

[12] Interesting footnote: Philip Pullman hates CS Lewis, because Lewis thought the best reward he could give the young heroes and heroines of his Narnia chronicles was that they should die before they leave the perfect, innocent world of childhood, and enter the messy, problematic world of adulthood. I loved the Narnia books as a child and didn't notice this weirdness at the time (if you do read them – and they're still great – you should start with *The Lion, the Witch and the Wardrobe*: it's the best one and was written first even though it's the second in the series). But I agree with Pullman that it's a horrible and immoral lesson to teach your readers. The point of all literature, children's or adults', is to help you grow up and lead a better life than the one you're leading now. So telling your young readers that death is better than adulthood (spoiler alert – it isn't) is a pretty major fail for a story.

until you've had a look at the true originals, the stories they read themselves as children, the ones that made them the storytellers they are; the old stories, where it all started.

How to pick a future classic

I've just bought Naomi Alderman's book *The Power*, published in 2017, because, from everything I've read about it, it looks like being a future classic. It's a science fiction novel about a world where all the women evolve to deliver electric shocks, like electric eels do when they're physically threatened, and how this changes that world. It could be a feminist sci-fi classic to put alongside *The Handmaid's Tale* or *Children of Men* or *Orlando* or *Frankenstein* or *The Blazing World*; and if you like any of these you might look at the (non-fiction) contributions to feminism of Mary Wollstonecraft (mother of Mary Shelley), John Stuart Mill, Laura Mulvey, Dale Spender, Mary Beard and Nina Power.

Maybe when I eventually read Naomi Alderman's book it won't be any good, and I'll be disappointed. But I doubt it. I'm rarely disappointed by the books I choose, because I always read several newspaper reviews online before I buy them. (Libraries exist – so use them, especially if you aren't sure whether you'll enjoy a book or not. Librarians exist, too, and can give you expert advice on what to read next. Equally, you're allowed to hang around in bookshops and spend ten minutes reading each and every book you think you might like. Unless you also happen to work there – which is why I got fired from Waterstones.)

Final thought on the Western canon

No one has read everything. And no one has time to, either. Google thinks there are 130,000,000 books in the world. The last person to have read every book ever published lived a long time ago, when that number was several zeroes shorter (it's impossible to know who that library-bothering individual was, but suggestions include the English poet Samuel Taylor Coleridge, the German philosopher Immanuel Kant, or the scientist Thomas Young (all 18th century), or the Ancient Greek philosopher-scientist Aristotle (fourth century BCE, so he would have had a much easier time of it).

So don't feel bad about not having read any particular book. Equally, if you're looking forward to finishing any book you have on the go, you might not be enjoying yourself. Maybe put it down and pick up another, even if you have to do an exam on it next week. Reading is, after all, supposed to be fun.

THE RIVER PROBLEM

Answer

So this question is about first understanding the three possible options you have at the beginning – which one of the fox, the goose or the beans to take across first? That trial and error process should eventually lead you to two insights. The first is easier than the second.

Insight One – you have to break the chain; you have to identify and remove the thing that interacts with both other elements. The fox only eats (the goose), and the sack of beans doesn't eat but is eaten (by the goose). On the other hand, the goose both eats and is eaten, so that has to go across first, to stop the other two from eating it/being eaten by it. The fox doesn't like beans, so you can safely leave those two alone together.

Insight Two – you have to go backwards to go forwards. It was hard even writing that, and when I say it out loud I normally get it the wrong way around. That's how unintuitive it is. (Much like the way that, when I mean to say I'm just thinking out loud, I actually say I'm just speaking out loud, which of course you're doing, because all speaking is speaking out loud.) But in this riddle, you really have to do this paradoxical thing: you really do have to go backwards in order to go forwards.

I think the second insight is harder because the first insight imposes a strict game world on you, one with just three choices at the beginning.

People I ask this question always want to tie up the fox so it doesn't get the goose, or stick the sack of beans in a tree so the goose can't get it. No. It's not a simulation. The fox, goose and beans aren't real – as evidence of that, there are many versions of this, dog/chicken/sack of grain and wolf/rabbit/cauliflower.

So it's a very limiting game with only three possible moves at the beginning, and it forces your thinking down very limited routes. And that's why it's so good. Because all creativity, whether you're solving problems or telling stories, needs limits; needs rules.

So, the solution: following the first insight, you take the goose across first, because the fox won't eat the beans. Then you row back, alone. Then, you take – it doesn't matter which – the fox or the beans across. Then – and here's the second insight in play, which is that you have to go back to go forwards – you take the goose – the problematic factor in all this, remember – back with you to the first bank. And then, whichever one of the fox or beans you left on the first bank, you take across to the second bank, leaving the goose alone on the first bank. So now the fox and the beans are both on the second bank, and all that remains for you to do is to row back to collect the goose, and bring it back to the second bank.

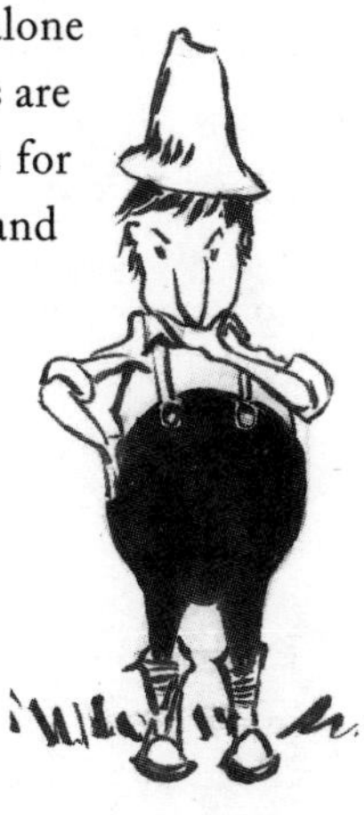

Mission completed!

2

HOW TO READ

Read what you like

So. The books in my lists in the previous chapter aren't necessarily the best books ever written, but they are the best ones I've ever read.

My advice is to pick any of these books that you like the sound of. Maybe stay out of the deep ends of the lists at first, unless a title grabs you. Then buy them, or better still, get someone else to buy them for you. Or, as I say, make use of your local public library. You can't write in library books, though.

You don't need to own every book you read, but lately I have tended to buy rather than borrow the ones I'm interested in because I like folding over pages and scribbling in my books when I'm moved to do so. If you did do that with library books, you'd just get a fine these days, but the playwright Joe Orton and his partner Keith Halliwell were sent to prison in the 1960s for (humorously) defacing books belonging to Islington Public Library. They're now on display at the Islington Local History Centre.

Reading is selfish

Forget million-minute book reading challenges. Reading is not a fun run. It's not something you do for charity, and it's not something you do for anyone else, either. Reading is, and should be, an entirely selfish activity. It should be done, ideally, completely alone.

Read every day, or all weekend, or perhaps before bed, whatever you want, as slow or fast as you want. Read *Diary of a Wimpy Kid*, or *The Power* or *Harry Potter*. Just please always bear in mind that there's other stuff out there, older stuff and that some of it – lots of it, to be honest – is better.

If you always read fast, read some poetry or something older to slow you down a bit – your comprehension might need fine tuning, and if not your comprehension, then your appreciation. Stories aren't just stories, you know. The point of a book is not to get to the end, like a race. The point is the time spent inhabiting another human's (or hobbit's) consciousness, and it should take as long as it takes, if not longer. You know you're reading the right book when the number of pages in your right hand dwindles to ten or fewer and you feel something in the pit of your stomach. Don't rush to the end: you can always re-read a book you love but you can't un-read it, you can't ever go back to reading it for the first time.

Give up

Here's what to do when your books arrive at your home,[13] or when you find your books in your local library.

First, read the first page or two of the book whose title might have passed briefly through your thoughts while you were waiting to read it.

Does it grab you?

If yes, keep going. You may want to sit down, but you do occasionally see people walking around towns and cities, nose buried in a book. Avoid if you live near a busy road; no book's worth dying for, I hope we can agree.

What if it doesn't grab you?

In that case, I strongly advise you to do something you probably don't do all that often, because you've been told (rightly) that if you do it all the time your life will suck.

---

[13] I realise the way I've phrased this assumes you'll be buying your books on Amazon – another nail in the coffin for bookshops. Actually, bookshops have one huge advantage over online behemoths, and it's that they don't stock every book in the world. They only have so much shelf space, so they only have the good ones – books chosen by people with expertise and taste. I particularly like the taste of the people who work in Daunt Books and Waterstones is really good these days too. Unfortunately, I've barely left the flat in the past four years – I've been writing this book – so it's been online shopping or nothing.

I want you to give up.

If you're not enjoying a book, give up. It'll still be there in ten years, by which time you'll be a different person, maybe the kind of person who'd enjoy such a book. But, for now, give up. Give yourself a break. But, while you're giving yourself a break, I want you to do something else. Something very important.

I want you to pick up another book.

Of all these books I'm recommending to you, I've only read about 90% of them to the end. The others I gave up on (too old, too long, too weird, too boring). I plan on going back to them sometime. I might die first, though. No rush.

It's not homework

Don't plough through books like they're homework. Bored of reading? Go next door and watch TV or go online or talk to another human being. There's plenty you can learn from them, too, if you ask the right questions.

Read any other books that you come across, if they take your fancy, or if someone you respect recommends them. And if you fall in love with one of those books, or indeed with one of the books on my lists, feel free to forget everything else and read everything they wrote. All the other dead authors, hoping you'll pick up their book, can just bloody well wait. Their turn will come. This list isn't a diet you should follow. It's a feast to gorge yourself on. So tuck in.

Mostly plants

Speaking of diets, the best diet advice I've heard, apart from Michael Pollan's seven-word mantra ('Eat food. Not too much. Mostly plants') is this: never eat anything your grandmother wouldn't recognise as food. (I think that's his too.) I take that as an argument in favour of recipes that generations of grandmothers have deemed worthy of passing on, like Chinese dan dan noodles or Italian *cacio e pepe*.

I'm here to tell you the same rule should apply to your reading habits: try to consume books you recognise as classics – either established, or possible future ones (cf. How to pick a future classic, p 64).

Avoid screens

When I was growing up you'd see the British Milk Council advertising milk. Milk! The same with the British Lamb and the British Beef Council. I'm not joking! These days, most food you see advertised on TV was invented in a laboratory by a transnational corporation and will give you diabetes. Same thing with books and screens. You hear a lot more about various portable electronic devices you can download novels on (among many other things), but no one's running global ad campaigns for the book. Books! They're cheap! Drop 'em in the bath, doesn't matter! Books! They can't do email! Books! No electricity needed – read 'em after civilisation collapses!

The thing about reading on a screen is, you always, in the background, have the possibility you could be reading something else. Something more interesting or immediately gratifying. It's like being in a conversation at a party where you're constantly looking over your conversation partner's shoulder for someone better to talk to. There's always someone better to talk to, in theory, and there's always something better to look at.

It's just that, well, it's a little rude. And you'll find it becomes hard to give even things you think you're interested in your full attention for more than a couple of minutes without getting distracted by something better, and a couple of minutes isn't enough time to really understand anything worth understanding.

A recent study has found there's a difference between how we read books, and how we read online. Our eyes move differently across books and screens. When we're reading a book, they move in an E-shape – left to right (assuming you're reading Western text), and line by line. Screens we read differently, in an F-shape. We read the first few lines carefully, then skim the rest along the left-hand margin. This suggests that our attention is much less focused when we're reading screens, and it certainly feels that way to me.

We have sourced information from books for millennia; screens for 20 years. So if you really want to focus on a piece of writing, print it out.

In this battle, you're up against the biggest companies ever, who make their money from getting your attention with pictures and words other people like you have made, and then putting advertisements next to them, for which other companies have paid. They want you to pay attention to them so that you buy those things, or, as in the supposed hacking of the 2016 American presidential election and the UK Brexit vote, because they want you to believe those things.

The behavioural scientist BF Skinner, whose work tech companies have used to make their devices addictive, said that 'For new behaviours to really take hold, they must occur often'.

So read every day. And consider not screening every day.

Bear in mind, finally, that the people who create these technologies don't let their children use them. Steve Jobs, when asked what his children thought of the iPad, said that they'd never used it. Silicon Valley executives don't let their children use social media, in much the same way as cigarette company executives don't smoke cigarettes. They know that, until around the age of 25, the human brain is still malleable, plastic – which both mean changeable.

And if you're over 25, and not responsible for any children's education, the point remains: Who do you want to be in charge of what goes into your brain? You, or someone else?

Age

At the age of about 30, most people stop listening to new kinds of music; they start to turn in on themselves, their tastes harden, they warp tight-shut, like old wooden doors. The same, I think, is true of books – why wouldn't it be? – and that's what I'm warning you against. It's certainly happened to me: I'm 40. It'll happen to you, too, if it hasn't already, so it's quite urgent, if you're still under 30, (not very urgent, but quite) that you take it upon yourself to fill your head now with the stuff that's going to be meaningful to you for the rest of your life. And if you're over 30, to force yourself to read new things.

I really do believe that education is what you remember after you've forgotten everything else. And if you want to be able to talk to other educated people, you should read some of the kinds of books on this list, which includes, as we have seen, a judicious number of books by dead people. That's what literature means: not just conversing with the dead, but conversing with them about other dead people. And not just with any dead people, but with some of the best,[14] most thoughtful people who ever lived.

John Keats wrote a poem 'On first looking into Chapman's Homer', about this. In it he expresses his bitter regret that he

[14] 'Best' in the intellectual sense mostly, because some of the ethically worst people have also made enduring contributions to civilisation, like the Italian Renaissance artist Caravaggio, who murdered someone.

hadn't read Homer (an eighth-century BCE poet) until he came across George Chapman's 1616 translation of Homer's two epic poems *The Iliad* (about the ten-year Trojan War) and *The Odyssey* (about the Greek hero Odysseus's ten-year journey home from that war to his wife Penelope). Keats wrote his poem in 1816, aged 21. He died aged 26. So, please bear in mind that, one way or another, you probably have less time than you think to find the books that will sustain you for the rest of your life.

Final thoughts

The older and larger the book, the older and larger you should probably be to get the most out of reading it. Ambition is great, but don't bite off more than you can chew – every book on my list is chewy enough already – and don't persevere unreasonably with any book you're not enjoying, or understanding.

It's not a marathon. It's not even a race, or any kind of competition. As I have said, you're not reading this book to finish it; quite the reverse. Some of my most melancholy moments have come in the last ten pages of a book I've loved. If you don't have that experience, you're probably reading the wrong books. Try something new, and don't let anyone put you down for enjoying a page-turner.

But be aware, too, that there's more out there than just page-turners.

As the writer Adam Gopnik says,

> I still think the greatest gift you can give kids is easy exposure to interesting things. Not compelling them to go see things, but making them feel that art and literature are just parts of the world.

And he writes for the *New Yorker*, so he would know.

SECOND QUESTION

THE TWO BEAKERS PROBLEM

You're a scientist in a laboratory. You have a beaker that holds exactly 300ml, and another beaker that holds exactly 500ml. Neither of them has any markings on them that could be used to measure any other quantity of liquid than these two quantities. You have a tap for water and a drain to throw away any excess water.

Can you use this equipment to measure out exactly 400ml? Obviously you can't just do it by eye – it wouldn't be exact enough. And you only have those two different-sized beakers.

How do you do it?

3

HOW TO WRITE

All writing is creative writing. The act of putting one word in front of another, whether you're writing a text message or an epic poem, means constantly making countless small choices. These are creative choices. And that's why writing well is hard, harder than anything else you might be asked to do at school, or outside it. Yes, harder than maths. Because maths is – at all but the highest levels of study – a simple, binary matter of getting it right or wrong. Maths is perfectible.

Writing is not. There's no perfect score in writing – 100%, at least in any meaningful way, is impossible. You might get an 'A', but you'll always know you could have done better. Even Shakespeare isn't necessarily worth 100%: he's just the best we've managed so far. The Koran, given that it was dictated to Muhammad by an omnipotent god, is perhaps worth 100%. But I think that proves my point. Writing well is hard; writing perfectly, without divine aid, is impossible.

I had an English teacher, Mr Nevin, who marked our weekly compositions out of 40, and I remember – after weeks of trying – finally hitting that perfect score, 40 out of 40, the *ne plus ultra*. At that moment, like Alexander the Great, I had no worlds left to conquer. Until I noticed my neighbour had scored 43. Out of 40. Mr Nevin had the eccentric, illogical but ultimately sensible policy of refusing to quantify that which cannot truly be quantified. A taskmaster of a teacher would have achieved this by simply setting a maximum of, say, 80%, above which he refused to ascend. But Mr Nevin's calculation was different: by making a numerical nonsense of his mark scheme, or at least an improper fraction, he was at once fulsomely encouraging our efforts while casting serious doubt on his or anyone else's right to so baldly assess the fruits of our brains. I still wanted to get beyond the 100% mark though. After all, as the English poet Robert Browning put it:

A man's reach should exceed his grasp,
Or what's a heaven for?

Perfection is impossible, then, for humans at least. You'll never better Shakespeare, let alone Allah. But this fact should encourage you. We may never reach the stars, not in my lifetime at least, but we can certainly navigate by them.

As the German poet and translator Michael Hofmann says:

> In English you always have to sound as if you are making an effort. English is basically a trap: class trap, dialect trap, feeling trap. It's almost a language for spies, for people to find out what people are really thinking.

Speaking as an Englishman myself, I can neither confirm nor deny this, but you could be forgiven for worrying that every time you open your mouth or put pen to paper, there's someone judging you. Because you'd be right. There is someone judging you, judging your every utterance and scribble. They're the harshest unkindest judge imaginable. That judge is you.

My advice is this. Don't write thinking about mistakes. In fact, don't even think about starting to write yet. There's something you need to do first.

Stage one: thinking

The what and the whom

Think about what you want to say, and to whom you want to say it. Knowing these two things should help you decide *how* to say it. Because form follows function, not the other way around. Thinking is planning, really, and we can go into that in the chapters on essays and stories, because how you plan a piece of writing depends on which of these two forms you're writing in.

But always consider this. Nearly everyone can speak well enough to express themselves. And most people can write, even if they write badly, well enough to express their thoughts, whatever they may be. But after that, when we consider how many people can really think, the field thins out considerably.

Which is why, before you start to write an essay – or story, or song, or any other piece of 'linked continuous writing' – you need to stop, really stop, and take a break. You might be doing your homework, you might be in an exam, you might be writing something for yourself – in which case this advice is even more important – because if no one's making you write this essay or story or song, then you really don't have any reason for not making it as good as it can possibly be.

Okay. Are you feeling focused? Then stop focusing. De-focus your mind, however worried you are. Stare out the window for a bit, or at your desk, or at the clock on the wall. Time passes pretty slowly when you're not doing anything, doesn't it, so don't worry about running out of it just yet. Now, just for a second, glance at the question you're supposed to answer, or the title you're working on. Now look away again. And look out the window again, or at the wall, all casual like.

Because there's still lots of time left, loads, and there's really nothing to worry about at all.

But, as we're here anyway, we might, I suppose, let the smallest corner of our minds drift towards the words at the top of our page, if we've even bothered to write it out a title yet, which maybe we haven't, because who cares, right?

> Wise men speak when they have something to say, fools speak because they have to say something.
> *Plato*

This is a bit harsh if you're in an exam – you have to say *something*, otherwise you'll get no marks for that question and probably fail the whole thing.

Quality, not quantity. How many books have you read that you never wanted to end? Very few, I'd have thought, and those were written by professional writers – who are probably, unless you're given to picking up obscure paperbacks in second-hand bookshops, among the most successful of all the professional writers, whose skill in holding a reader's attention has sold hundreds of thousands or even millions of books.

Now, with respect, you're probably not a professional writer, but you do have something in common with them: you're going to sit there in silence for an uncomfortably long time, before you even think about where your pen is, and just *think* about exactly what it is you want to say. And when you do eventually start to write, from a plan you've scribbled on a scrap in a way that works for you, you're going to use as few words as possible to make the most meaning you can. So *please* don't write too much. You might reasonably suggest I take my own advice – I've been rambling on this topic for quite a while now. Two thoughts on that: one, if you're getting annoyed by my wordiness, imagine how much worse it would be if I didn't have an important point to make; and two, please bear in mind that this book is 50,000 words long, and that I wrote more than twice that before cutting the worst of my rambling. Like I said, it could have been much, much worse.

Think of it this way. How many really great pop songs are longer than seven minutes? 'Marquee Moon' by Television. 'Blue Monday' by New Order. 'The Payback' by James Brown. 'The Message' by Grandmaster Flash. 'Purple Rain' by Prince. 'I Am the Resurrection' by the Stone Roses. 'Jump into the Fire' by Harry Nilsson is exactly seven minutes. That's about it. 'Being Boring' by the Pet Shop Boys and 'Ike's Mood' by Isaac Hayes are both just under. Sorry.

And how many great songs are under three minutes long? Thousands. John Ruskin, the 19th-century writer, said:

> Quality is never an accident. It is always the result of intelligent effort.

Or as our old friend Aristotle put it: 'Quality is not an act, it is a habit.' But most of all, quality means thinking about *what you really want to say.*

The what

If you're thinking about what you're going to write, this should take about *a third of your total writing time*, at least to begin with. You can make rough notes, a few words or phrases scribbled on a piece of scrap paper, connected by arrows, anything to convey your ideas to the future you who will soon be putting pen to paper. But NO FULL SENTENCES. Not yet.

In the earliest days of professional football, coaches would train all week without the ball, in the expectation that the players would be hungrier for it, and therefore play better, in the match on Saturday. That, of course, was a terrible idea. If you want to excel at something, you're better off practising *the actual thing you want to excel at*. But I can't help liking the logic.

When you're writing, hold yourself back from starting for as long as possible. You need to think first, then examine your thoughts – because as William James put it 'A great many people think they are thinking when they are merely rearranging their prejudices'. Then, when you've used up approximately *one third of the allocated time*, you can start writing.

The whom

Planning also means thinking about *whom you want to say it to*. Often, we'll know who is going to read what we write: letter, email, homework. But sometimes we don't know who'll read it: the examiner who'll mark your English exam, the person who'll read the book I'm writing now. Either way, though, we know something about that person, even if we don't know who they are.

An examiner is someone who loves their subject so much they decided to dedicate their life to teaching it. But right now they are spending their summer holiday reading and marking, according to strict guidelines, a hundred similar exam scripts, for not enough money. You'd do well to empathise with them. What do they want from you? They want you to rekindle their own flagging enthusiasm by demonstrating your own insight into and appreciation of the text: they want you to say something no one else has said that makes them slap their sweating forehead and say, *at last: someone who gets it.*

My reader, I think, and I'm talking about you here, is someone who wants to learn something and is doing it, at least partly, off your own back. Someone might have bought this book for you – but you're probably not reading it entirely under duress. It's pretty hard to make someone read something they don't want to, and I know this having been on both sides of that struggle. I don't know my reader's age, but you're almost certainly older than ten, and probably older than 12. Maybe you're a lot older, in your 20s or 40s or 50s. When I'm tutoring I talk to my students as if they're adults. With this person, therefore, I'm going to assume that I can't assume the things they do and don't know. But I know they're motivated so I'll try not to repeat myself and bore them.

My other advice is this: find your voice. Or tone, or register. Your spoken voice changes naturally, depending on whom you're speaking to, and so should your written voice.

For example, I would've said the less formal but less correct 'on who' instead of 'on whom' just then if I were speaking out loud, and I wouldn't've used so many abbreviations or 'I's in a more formal piece.

There's an old test you can apply to a newspaper columnist's writing, which is to count the number of sentences with 'I' in them, and divide by the total number of sentences. The higher the percentage, the more self-obsessed the writer. Doesn't look too good for *your author*, does it? *One* wonders if there's any way around this embarrassing problem.

Stage two: writing

Write like you speak

Try to write like you speak – it's what I try to do, and it seems to work... I've written a book, after all. Well, I'm writing one. It's not for nothing that authors are said to have a voice, and that promising but not-quite-there writers are told: 'Find your voice'. Perhaps the ideal scenario is what Dorothy finds in *The Wizard of Oz* – that it's inside you all along. Here's hoping.

The more I think about it the more I think punctuation is the key to all this – that at the very least, punctuation is the frame you paint inside. I've been deliberately sloppy with it in these past two paragraphs, and I think that sloppiness somehow represents my speech most truthfully. In speaking I often meander and (yes) pause, these pauses often coming, mid clause, where they shouldn't.

Forebears

As with deceased relatives' belongings, keep what you like and leave the rest. Read widely, and when you're not reading widely, read deeply.

I spent a year devouring, and then consuming, and finally chewing sullenly over almost everything F Scott Fitzgerald wrote. The wonder of him is that his first three novels were enormous hits, read by 20 million 'sad young men' when

America was only 120 million souls. And, well, they just weren't very good.

And then, despite all that success, he wrote his fourth novel, *The Great Gatsby*, which for my money was the best one written in English in the 20th century. Re-reading a book that speaks to you is perhaps the best way of learning how your pages can be made to speak to others.

Speak as you like

Incidentally, if you can write in different registers, or voices, you can speak in them, too.

In the end all writing is – or should be – ventriloquism, because you're never writing in your own voice but in the voice of someone who is cleverer and kinder and funnier and wiser than you. At least that's what you're aiming for.

Learning a new voice, or accent, is a good idea because it is:

1. Not that hard to do if you can amuse yourself with it; and
2. A lot easier than actually learning a foreign language.

My advice is to watch Cary Grant films – here's a man, from the mean streets of Bristol's Hotwells, who entirely created his own voice, and became the greatest male movie star of his day (if you've seen George Clooney, great as he is, you've seen but an imitation of Cary Grant). A couple of Cary Grant quotes to clarify this point:

Everyone wants to be Cary Grant. Even I want to be Cary Grant.

I pretended to be somebody I wanted to be until finally I became that person. Or he became me.

The point is, that you're driving this car. You can pick and choose. One year I decided I was going to laugh like Sid James from the Carry On films (it's a very dirty laugh), and now I'm stuck with it. Serves me right. *Ah-ha-ha-ha.*

Speak like you write

Mr Wyke, one of my many stellar English teachers, once told our class that, whenever he spoke, in his mind's eye he saw the words appear in print, all perfectly punctuated. It was as if he were reading from a teleprompter; or, more accurately, as if he were his own stenographer, studiously recording on an imaginary page every phrase he uttered.

When I tell you to write like you speak, I'm not encouraging you to fret over punctuation every time you open your mouth. Rather, I want you to listen with care to the rhythms of your speech – where do you naturally pause in your sentences? Try to reproduce – and sensitively punctuate – those rhythms on the page.

Mistakes

As I said, don't write worrying about mistakes. That's what stage three is for. And don't write worrying about time. When it comes to essay writing, you know how long you have – it's exactly the same amount of time you took at stage one to think and plan your piece. Yes, I'm giving you *one third of your allocated time* to do the actual writing part of your writing. So you'd better have thought through what you want to say in some detail beforehand.

If you imagine your mind during stage one as a greyhound in her starting box just before a race, you want to spend lots of time building up tension – these are the thoughts and feelings you generate when you think and plan and debate with yourself about what you really want to say to your reader – because then the writing goes faster, and easier.

So, don't worry about mistakes. Just write. You can fix the rest later. Except for two things: paragraphs and sentences. I'm assuming you're writing by hand here, which (even if you don't have to) is worth doing because it's a high-wire act that will make you a better writer. Think about it. Without a word-processing programme, you don't have the safety net of a spellchecker, and even more perilously, you can't cut and paste phrases or move paragraphs. It forces you to think hard about what you want to say, and the proper order for those thoughts.

Paragraphs

The only rules about when to start a new paragraph are these: when you change the subject, when you change the speaker in a dialogue between two or more people and when you change the time or place.

My only rule about new paragraphs is this: if I feel like I *might* need a new paragraph, I probably *do*.

It's never served me badly, that rule, though obviously a lot of one-sentence paragraphs in (say) a history essay might suggest that I don't know much detail and I'm covering up for it with a flashy style. Three or four sentences are usually enough to get your point across, anyway, though reading back what I've written so far, I do occasionally run to five or six.

A very short paragraph is not at all a bad thing, as long as you mix it up with longer ones.

And that goes double for *sentence length*. Here are the thoughts of ace writing teacher Gary Provost:

> This sentence has five words. Here are five more words. Five-word sentences are fine. But several together become monotonous. Listen to what is happening. The writing is getting boring. The sound of it drones. It's like a stuck record. The ear demands some variety.
>
> Now listen. I vary the sentence length, and I create music. Music. The writing sings. It has a pleasant rhythm, a lilt, a harmony. I use short sentences. And I use sentences

of medium length. And sometimes, when I am certain the reader is rested, I will engage him with a sentence of considerable length, a sentence that burns with energy and builds with all the impetus of a crescendo, the roll of the drums, the crash of the cymbals, sounds that say: listen to this, it is important.

These two things – your paragraphs and your sentences and how you vary their lengths – together create the rhythms of your writing, and while you can mess around with those rhythms afterwards when you edit your work, life's much easier when you get them right first time.

There's a third thing. Repetition. By which I mean repetition of words, not repetition of ideas. If you keep repeating the same words, your reader will get bored. Repeating an *idea* is often necessary because, in a paragraph about, for example, repetition, you're going to have to refer to the *concept* of repetition several times to get your *point* across. But try not to repeat the word itself – for example, the word 'repetition' – repeatedly, because too much repetition can get… repetitive.

I can think of three possible ways out of this: using pronouns (assuming it's a noun you're trying to avoid repeating), using synonyms and using circumlocutions. For example, Milton's *Paradise Lost* is one of the longer poems in the English language, and its hero/villain/anti-hero Satan gets named a lot. How does Milton avoid using the S-word too much? By using pronouns ('He'), synonyms ('Lucifer') and circumlocutions ('the Enemy of Man') instead.

On the other hand, repetition, of words or ideas, can sometimes be the best way of getting your point across. Simply reiterating an idea forces it into people's heads. Churchill said that repeating yourself is the only rhetorical trick that actually works:

> If you have an important point to make, don't try to be subtle or clever. Use a pile driver. Hit the point once. Then come back and hit it again. Then hit it a third time – a tremendous whack.

It's also said that, when we hear an animal repeat itself, whether it's a bird or a whale, we call that singing. That's true of humans too. It's why songs have choruses – we like to hear the best bits repeated.

You can't get it right first time. So try and get right the things that are hardest to fix. For everything else, there's…

Stage three: editing

As Ernest Hemingway said, the first draft of anything is shit. He won the Nobel Prize for Literature and presumably knows what he's talking about. Here are four things to think about as you look over your work. In exams, you're often told to spend the last five minutes checking. I'd like you, at least to start with, to spend a third of your total time checking your work. Having spent decades marking my own and my students' work, I spot a mistake on the page like a hawk spies a mouse in a field – and so will you, if you take more time over it now.

Decimation

My first piece of advice isn't to do with mistakes per se, but with excess. Brevity is the soul of wit. See if you can see what I'm getting at. You don't have to do this exercise every time (unless you're writing a book, in which case bad luck), but if you try it occasionally you'll have a new tool in your box.

When an ancient Roman regiment rebelled against its leader, the Romans would put the rebellion down, and then they would do something rather cunning. Instead of *annihilating* everyone in the regiment (*ad nihil*, literally 'to nothing'), or indeed *deleting* the regiment itself (*deleo, delere, delui, deletum*, 'to destroy'), they would do something called *decimation*, which doesn't mean what most people think it means. Decimation, like decimals, and decagons, has to do with doing things in tens. What the ancient Romans did was this: they'd line up all the men in the rebellious regiment and the centurion would walk down the line with his sword drawn, counting the men. Every time he got to ten, the centurion would stop. He would kill the man standing there, and then start counting again from one.

Now, when you're running your own regiment, I'd warn you off this kind of collective punishment: it's unjust, because it punishes people who weren't necessarily involved, and it's imprecise, because you're not actually getting the ringleaders – you're terrorising everyone, which I'm afraid was the point (the Romans, by today's standards, weren't terribly nice). Words aren't people, though, so we don't really need to worry about their feelings as we hack them up. More than that, we're not picking the words we decimate randomly, without any thought. Instead, we're trying to remove the words *whose absence won't affect the meaning of those that remain*. Because if we do that, the effect of those meaningful words will be more powerful, less diluted by the meaningless ones.

We all know people who make everyone groan when they tell jokes because they include so many irrelevant details that you're too tired to laugh when they finally get to the punchline. Or, as the French mathematician and philosopher Blaise Pascal said 'I'm sorry I wrote you such a long letter: I didn't have time to write a shorter one'. With this in mind, let's try that exercise again.

When an ancient Roman regiment rebelled against its leader, they would put the rebellion down, and then they would do something rather cunning. Instead of *annihilating* everyone in the regiment (*ad nihil*, literally 'to nothing'), or deleting the regiment itself (*deleo*, *delere*, *delui*, *deletum*, 'to destroy'), they would do something called *decimation*, which doesn't mean what most people think . Decimation, like decimals, and decagons, has to do with doing things in tens. What the Romans did was line up all the men in the regiment, and the centurion would walk with his sword drawn, counting them . Every time he got to ten, the centurion would kill the man standing there, and then start counting again from one.

Now, when you're running your own regiment, I'd warn you off this kind of collective punishment: it's unjust, because it punishes people who weren't involved, and it's imprecise, because you're not getting the ringleaders – you're terrorising everyone, which I'm afraid was the point (the Romans, by today's standards, weren't terribly nice). Words aren't people, though: don't worry about their feelings . More than that, we're not picking the words we decimate randomly . Instead, we remove the words *whose absence won't affect the meaning of those that remain*. Because if we do that, the effect of those meaningful words will be less diluted by the meaningless ones.

We all know people who make everyone groan when they tell jokes because they include so many irrelevant details before they get to the punchline. Or, as the French mathematician and philosopher Blaise Pascal said, 'I'm sorry I wrote you such a long letter: I didn't have time to write a shorter one.'

Very and really and !!

Two words that often deserve decimation are 'really' and 'very'. Really? Very much so. Why? Well, they're called intensifiers, which means they modify – and in theory intensify – the adjectives they describe.

'I'm really happy to be here' – are you? You don't sound it. Read that sentence again, aloud. You might even sound sarcastic, depending on your tone. Or – instead – are you ecstatic, chuffed to bits, made up? Likewise 'He's nice' is promising, if a bit weak (there are nicer words than nice). Yet somehow, 'He's very nice...' is always anticipating a '...but...'

As I've already said,[15] adding unnecessary words nearly always weakens your meaning, by diluting it. So avoid needless verbiage, even/especially if you're trying to jazz up a sentence – which, if that's your plan, well, try choosing a better word, a clearer or more fun one, or chuck in a short punchy sentence; you can even knock two sentences into one with a deft semicolon like this.

Intensifier is a misnomer, then – 'really' and 'very' don't really intensify anything. Some words don't do exactly what it

[15] And I now unnecessarily repeat.

says on the tin. A few do the exact opposite. Every language has them. Even my second favourite one, Italian.[16]

Other unhelpful adornments

1. Exclamation marks are like laughing at your own joke, as F Scott Fitzgerald said. It's a cheap trick; it doesn't work. Not that I'm against cheap tricks if they do. If you want to surprise your reader, try writing a sentence without a verb:

> A arse-aching dawn.
> For sale: baby shoes, never worn.
> A squat grey building of only thirty-four stories.[17]

2. Any word other than 'said' used after direct speech.

'Really?' you enquire.

'Yes,' I say.

The words inside the speech marks should do all the heavy lifting. Agonise over them instead. 'Ask' and 'reply' can be tolerated, I suppose, especially if you're Ring Lardner:

---

[16] In his brilliant *Unreliable Memoirs*, Australian polymath Clive James has to get out of the Italian city Piacenza quick. Hobbled by a broken ankle, he's also pissed off some local toughs. Our hero boards a fast-sounding *treno accelerato* to Florence, but it transpires that *accelerato* is the Italian word for 'stopping at every station and going very slowly in between so as not to overshoot'.

[17] I'm not going to give you these sources; Google any lines you like.

Are you lost daddy I arsked tenderly.

Shut up he explained.

The injunction on 'said' is Raymond Chandler's, another tough-minded American (the great crime novelist, ahead of Agatha Christie). Watch his films noirs, *The Big Sleep* and *Double Indemnity*. Feel the rub of that rough, perfect dialogue said out loud:

Walter: So you lie awake in the dark and listen to him snore and get ideas.

Phyllis: Walter, I don't want to kill him. I never did. Not even when he gets drunk and slaps my face.

Walter: Only sometimes you wish he was dead.

Phyllis: Perhaps I do.

Walter: And you wish it was an accident and you had that policy for $50,000 dollars. Is that it?

Phyllis: Perhaps that too.

Which six words should come after these six speeches? Try sticking in 'he speculated'/'she protested'/'he suggested'/'she conceded'/'he enquired'/'she agreed'. Makes sense at least. But it's terrible. It's like the frame is trying to outshine the picture. No. You're the frame. Do your job. The correct answer is 'he said'/'she said'/'he said'/'she said'/'he said'/'she said'. In fact you only need the first 'he said'/'she said'. It's just the two of them talking, the life insurance salesman and the unhappy wife.

3. Dotting i's with circles (I did this for a year when I was 14. Ugh.)

4. Using blue ink (A few years ago I switched to black. I take my words more seriously in monochrome. So will you. Any colour as long as it's black.)

5. All unhelpful adornments (Let words speak for themselves.)

A warning

Don't decimate everything you write – it's exhausting, and boring. This is an exercise to help you get into the habit of meaningful brevity, but it can go too far. The Roman poet Horace complained that:

> *brevis esse laboro; obscurus fio*
> I try to be brief; I become obscure

Keep the words you need or you'll stop making sense. There's a (probably apocryphal) story about a New York journalist who flew to Los Angeles to interview Cary Grant, but realised on his return that he'd forgotten to ask him an important question. So he sent him a telegram, making it as brief as possible because telegrams were charged by the word:

HOW OLD CARY GRANT?

The reply came immediately:

OLD CARY GRANT FINE. HOW YOU?

Writing is a habit

Obviously, you won't write the way you want to immediately. Practice helps. What I aim for is 300 words a day. A professional writer once told me that's pathetic – I should aim for 500–1000 words per day. But the fact of doing it every day is much more important than the amount you write. (And whenever a student hands me reams of work, my heart sinks, because I know it will not have been thought through, and it'll be lousy with errors.)

Describing things you've seen, or thoughts you've had, in clear and characterful English, is as useful a writing exercise as I can think of.

Yes. I'm asking you to keep a diary.

THE TWO BEAKERS PROBLEM

Answer

If at any point while reading this explanation – which will be pretty drawn out to allow for these moments of inspiration – you start to think about possible answers to the problem, then stop reading and start thinking for yourself.

This problem actually has a similar structure to the River Problem, and it's solved the same way – via trial and error. It's all very well being wise after you've seen the solution – don't read ahead; this moment of uncertainty is where you need to be right now: if I could, I'd set up shop here permanently – but the way you get to any solution is by failure or, more precisely, a logical, organised process where you learn from your failures.

So what are your options? You have two options. Fill one of the two beakers to the top. Which one? Does it matter? Let's say you fill the 500ml one. Now what? You have three options. Empty the 500ml beaker. Fill the 300ml beaker. Or fill the 300ml beaker from the 500ml beaker.

The First Insight is this: there's a difference in volume between the two beakers, and you can use that. Let's recap.

Fill the 500ml beaker. From that beaker, fill the 300ml one. You now have 200ml in the big beaker. You're halfway there.

200ml is halfway to 400ml, which you're trying to get, right? But actually you're not halfway there. Because you can't just repeat that step to get another 200ml, add them together, and get 400ml. Because where do you put the first 200ml? You needed both beakers free to get that first 200ml, so you can't just repeat the same steps to get the second 200ml you need. Because you don't have a third beaker to put the first 200ml in, and you need both beakers free to get the second 200ml you need to get to 200ml + 200ml = 400ml. So you haven't quite cracked it yet.

But, by pouring the 300ml beaker into the 500ml beaker, leaving a known 200ml of space in the larger beaker, you've changed the capacity of that beaker. And that's the Second Insight.

So now, all you need to do is to refill the 300ml beaker, then carefully pour it into the 500ml beaker – which already contains 300ml, and can therefore only take another 200ml from the smaller beaker. You're left with 100ml in the 300ml beaker. The 500ml beaker is full.

Empty the 500ml beaker. Pour the 100ml from the small beaker into the big one. Refill the small beaker. Pour that 300ml from the small beaker into the larger one, which already contains 100ml. What does that make?

100ml + 300ml = 400ml.

Mission accomplished!

4

HOW TO STRUCTURE AN ESSAY

Stage one: Hegel, or disagreeing with yourself

It's *traditional* to begin an essay by defining your terms. So – what is an essay?

An essay, from the French *essayer* meaning to attempt, is an *attempt* to answer a question. Your attempt at a response to an essay question will be – and should be – at once personally felt and logically argued, but it will not, and cannot be a definitive and final answer. So don't worry about it too much. No one expects you to knock 'Is there a God?' on the head, once and for all time, in 45 minutes. The Swiss German artist Paul Klee said that 'A line is just a dot going for a walk'. Well, an essay is just your brain going for a walk.

Binary opposition = conflict

Like I said, the *traditional* way to begin an essay is by defining your terms. The best way, though, is to start off by setting up a *binary opposition* between two opposing arguments. Binary just means there are two things, as in the word bicycle (= two circles, aka wheels) or binoculars (= two eyes). And opposition means that those two things are on opposing sides. Basically, you want to set two opposite ideas against each other, and make them fight it out. Let them do the work for you.

Notice the way I just did exactly that: by setting the *traditional* method (of beginning an essay by defining your terms) up against the best one (this method of binary opposition), I've already generated conflict. This principle of conflict is most often used when telling stories (in a story, someone always wants something badly, and someone or something is stopping them from getting it – which is what conflict is). But, if anything, conflict is even more crucial for essays.

Binary versus open-ended questions

So, there are two kinds of essay question: questions that contain a binary opposition, and those that don't, which are *open-ended*. The best kind is binary, which (much like this sentence which says there are only two kinds of essay) suggests there are two – and only two – sides to any argument.

Notice, again, how I've turned the above paragraph into an argument between the two different kinds of question:

that's another binary opposition right there. Here are some examples of questions that contain a binary opposite:

- Is there a God?
- Should we have a death penalty?
- Is Satan the hero of *Paradise Lost*?

Basically, if you can answer a question with either a yes or a no, like these ones and many others, then you're in luck.

Unfortunately for me, though, this essay question – How do I write an essay? – is the other kind, open-ended. Look back at the title I've set myself. (I advise you to do this after every paragraph, when you're writing your own essays, to keep you on track – always ATQ: Answer The Question.) Can this particular essay question be answered with a simple yes or no? No it can't. So it's open-ended, like these ones:

- What's the meaning of life?
- What were the causes of the First World War?
- How do I write an essay? (for some reason, this one's weighing on my mind)

Looks like I've got my work cut out.

Essay planning – binary questions

This is such a straightforward joy, I'm going to give it to you in numbered steps.

1 Take a piece of paper
2 Draw a line down the middle
3 Write the binary title at the top

4 Write pro (Latin for 'for') and contra ('against') on either side of the line; if you want to be even more straightforward you can just write 'yes' and 'no'

5 Then put your pen down, look at the title you've just written, and really think quite hard about it for quite a long time

6 Do you agree or disagree with the statement, or a bit of both?

7 Why?

8 Pick up your pen and write down all the reasons why, or why not, in the appropriate column

9 Bravo/a, you've just written a competent essay plan.

Here's an example of a pros and cons essay plan. In the second episode of the TV show *Breaking Bad*, Chemistry teacher-turned-criminal Walter White has to decide what to do with Krazy-8, a rival criminal who is trapped in his basement. Like any educated man, Walter weighs up the pros and cons: as with any good essay title, there are only two binary choices to decide between.

SHOULD I KILL KRAZY-8?

Let him live (contra)	**Kill him (pro)**
It's the moral thing to do Judeo/Christian principles You are not a murderer Sanctity of life	HE'LL KILL YOUR ENTIRE FAMILY IF YOU LET HIM GO

Even though the 'Let him live' column outweighs the 'Kill him' column by four points to one, Walter ends up killing the rival criminal. This is entirely logical. Always bear in mind that it's not just the number of arguments you can make for or against any given proposition, it's how strong those arguments are all combined. You are the ultimate decider; the pros and cons list, and the essay itself, are just a way to compel you to consider both sides of the argument before you make up your mind.

In this case, Walter decides to take one life in order to save several lives (they are also the lives of the people closest to him). One might argue with Walter's assumption that the criminal will kill his family, but not with his final assessment: that one argument is stronger than the other four put together.

Here's another pros and cons list, by another scientist, Charles Darwin, to help him make another big life decision:

SHOULD I GET MARRIED?

Marry (pro)	**Not marry (contra)**
Children (if it please God)	Freedom to go where one liked
Constant companion, (& friend in old age) who will feel interested in one	Choice of Society & little of it
	Conversation of clever men at clubs

Continued...

Marry (pro)

Object to be beloved & played with

Better than a dog anyhow

Home, & someone to take care of house

Charms of music & female chit-chat

These things good for one's health

But terrible loss of time

My God, it is intolerable to think of spending one's whole life, like a neuter bee, working, working, & nothing after all

No, no won't do

Imagine living all one's day solitarily in smoky dirty London House

Only picture to yourself a nice soft wife on a sofa with good fire, & books & music perhaps

Compare this vision with the dingy reality of Grt. Marlbro' St

Not marry (contra)

Not forced to visit relatives, & to bend in every trifle

To have the expense & anxiety of children

Perhaps quarrelling

Loss of time

Cannot read in the evenings

Fatness & idleness

Anxiety & responsibility, less money for books &c

If many children forced to gain one's bread.

(But then it is very bad for one's health to work too much)

Perhaps my wife won't like London; then the sentence is banishment & degradation into indolent, idle fool —

Darwin ended up marrying his cousin Emma Wedgwood and had ten children with her. Though three of them died young, he doesn't seem to have regretted his decision.

Essay planning – open-ended questions

For an open-ended question, you should write a different kind of essay plan. This is the spider chart, in which your ideas grow outwards, like arachnid legs, from the open-ended question at its centre (the spider's body). You can also call it a mind map, but I prefer to call it a spider chart, because I dislike spiders nearly as much as I dislike open-ended essay questions, so the term seems appropriate. Here is a very simple example of one:

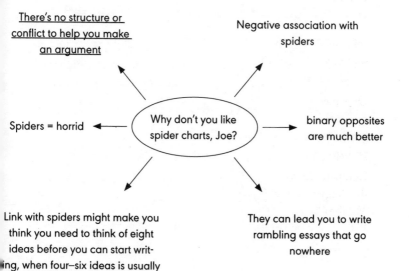

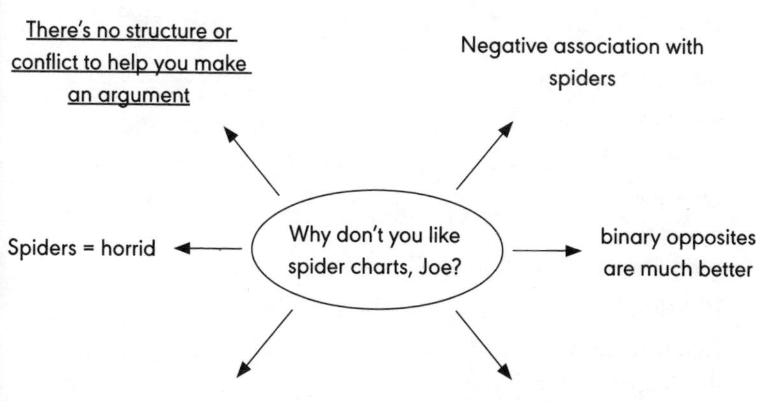
Why don't you like spider charts, Joe?
There's no structure or conflict to help you make an argument
Negative association with spiders
Spiders = horrid
binary opposites are much better
Link with spiders might make you think you need to think of eight ideas before you can start writing, when four–six ideas is usually enough for the average essay
They can lead you to write rambling essays that go nowhere

The main point in this essay plan is the one I've underlined: the lack of a clear back-and-forth argument means essays written from spider charts can often end up being unstructured and unfocused. You have to work really hard to keep to the point of the title. (You might have noticed that I'm having that exact problem right now.)

Can I take this opportunity, while we both take a quick breather, to ask you a question? What have you taken from this essay so far? Without looking back a page? It's binary versus open-ended, isn't it? That's because I disagreed with myself. Because there was conflict between these opposing ideas. 'Out of the quarrel with ourselves we make poetry,' said the Irish poet WB Yeats.

Hegel, dialectic and disagreeing with yourself

Two hundred years ago, a German philosopher called Georg Wilhelm Friedrich Hegel was thinking about how arguments get resolved and came up with the idea of 'dialectic'. Dialectic comes from the same Greek word root as dialogue, which means two people talking. But instead of two people, Hegel imagined two ideas talking to each other, and disagreeing. These two ideas are opposing (or opposite) ideas, and so they naturally disagree, which causes our old friend conflict. Hegel called the two opposing ideas in a dialectic by the names thesis and antithesis.

What happens during the process of dialectic is that thesis

and antithesis battle it out until they've knocked all the wrong stuff out of each other, and are so exhausted by the effort that their battered remains kind of melt into each other, to create an entirely new thing, synthesis, which is made up of the best bits of both thesis and antithesis, the right stuff that's left over from the battle.

And this is what you're doing in your binary essay – you're taking your two columns of opposing ideas, and making them battle it out, one at a time. And what you're left with, whatever survives, is your synthesis – your final answer to the question at the top of the page.

Marx: capitalism versus communism

For an example of dialectic I'm going to use Hegel's greatest student, Karl Marx, who applied this process of dialectic to history. Marx lived during the Industrial Revolution, when many people worked in factories making things to sell. Because these factories were owned by their bosses, the things these people made were then taken by the bosses and sold, which made the bosses rich. But the people who had made these things were paid very little, much less than the things they had made were worth. All work, whether in factories or in any other job, was organised this way, with the bosses owning the means of production, and the workers being paid less than their work was worth so the bosses could take most of the profits. Marx called this system capitalism.

Marx believed that it was wrong for these few bosses to be rich while the many workers were poor, even though it was their work that made the bosses rich. He proposed that the government take over the ownership of the factories from the bosses, and that the money made from selling the things they produced be shared equally among the workers who did the work. This system was called communism.

Marx wrote a book, *Capital*, which described the existing system that only benefited the bosses, and *The Communist Manifesto,* which described how he thought things ought to be. These two books define the thesis and antithesis which, over the past 150 years, have been fighting it out – battling over the question of how the world should be run – both in the politics within countries and in the wars between them. The communist countries collapsed in 1991, which seemed to give victory to the capitalist ones, but then they partially collapsed themselves in 2008, so neither side has completely triumphed.

What has happened, though, over these 150 years, is that each side has moved closer to the other, with the capitalist countries of Western Europe adopting ideas from communism, such as the nationalisation (taking over by the government) of certain industries. In Britain, for example, we have a National Health Service run by the government which is free for everyone; in France the railways are run by the government, and so on – even though these are still mostly capitalist countries. So, even though there is no final answer between these two arguments, there are signs that a kind of synthesis – or agreement – between the original thesis (capitalism) and antithesis (communism) is taking shape.

My point in all this is not to persuade you which of these two sides is the right one, although you might be able to guess, from how I presented them both, which side I have more sympathy with (and please do bear in mind that the way you present an argument affects how much people are convinced by it – this will be important later). All I want to do here is to show you that laying out your pro and contra arguments next to each other, and having them fight it out, is the only way to write an essay, because it's the only way you can get to an answer, or a synthesis, to the question you're asking yourself.

This synthesis is the point of Hegel's dialectic: two ideas talking until they come to some kind of agreement. And this is how it works, or is supposed to work, in Parliament – whose name comes from a French word, *parler*, which also means talking – where the two sides argue until a compromise (or synthesis) is reached. They don't know how it's going to go until the end.

For the ancient Chinese philosopher Confucius, harmony and peace are made by consensus and compromise, not by blind conformity. Consensus and compromise require loyal opposition – people willing to argue in favour of opposing ideas. A country is at risk, Confucius said, when a prince believes that 'the only joy in being a prince is that no one opposes what one says'.

On being in two minds

Some advice on generating content: if you get stuck halfway through a paragraph, there are worse options than simply starting a new paragraph with the words 'On the other hand…' – and then finding reasons to violently disagree with what you've just said. Counterargument is a technique that makes you look fair-minded. As F Scott Fitzgerald says:

> The test of a first-rate intelligence is the ability to hold two opposed ideas in the mind at the same time...

For this reason, you should start and end an essay with your second-best and best points – it's more exciting.

The German philosopher Hannah Arendt said that in order to judge, we must take into account the perspectives of others, to imagine what they may think or feel – to adopt what she called 'an enlarged mentality'.

That's what an essay is – considering both sides. Or at least considering other possibilities, other perspectives, counterarguments that test your initial thoughts.

By the way, these rules – like the models that explain the world, and in doing so oversimplify it and thus distort it to make it comprehensible to us – are only to be used until you find better rules, at which point, discard them like rusty tricycles without a backward glance.

Whatever you think, think the opposite

Why should you do this? Two reasons. One – by trying to think of a counterargument for each point that occurs to you, you double the number of points you generate. One point, properly developed/explored, means one paragraph. You can easily get four paragraphs from two ideas this way.

Two – it generates conflict. Conflict is essential in story telling, where the ending has been decided already by the storyteller, and in sport, where the final result hasn't been pre-decided and the two sides battle it out live. Conflict's also crucial in argumentative essay-writing. The whole point of dialectic is that it's a conflict between two opposed ideas. But it's more than that: like in a story or a football match, it's the conflict between two sides – and the uncertainty of the outcome – that keeps your reader interested.

So, keep them guessing. Space your points out, don't give away your final decision until the end. Maybe odd-numbered paragraphs should support the proposition in the essay's title, and even-numbered paragraphs could contradict it (only roughly, though – you don't need to go crazy over this. It's just an easy template to remember). It should look like a hard-fought tennis point, each player countering their opponent's last move using all their strength, or like an end-to-end football match where both teams look like scoring a decisive goal until the last minute. A football match that's 4-0 at half time then 4-3 at full time is less thrilling than one that goes 0-1, then 2-1, then 2-3, then 4-3. You can then decide in your final paragraph – or just in a masterful final sentence – which of the points you've already made have been decisive, and declare a winner on that basis. Save the best till last.

On disagreeing with yourself

Here are some thoughts, from much more intelligent people than me, on the subject of disagreeing with yourself:

> A great many people think they are thinking when they are merely rearranging their prejudices.
> *William James, American psychologist*

> When the facts change, I change my mind.
> *John Maynard Keynes, English economist*

> Thinking hard should make your head hurt.
> *Mary Beard, English classicist*

> Whatever you think, think the opposite.
> *Paul Arden, a former advertising director at Saatchi & Saatchi (This is the title of his good, fun and very short book)*

A lot of communists changed their mind about communism when the truth came out about Stalin's gulags, the Siberian prison camps in which 10-20 million people died because he saw them as a threat to communism. So it's fine to change your mind between the start and the end of an essay. It's more than fine, actually – it's a sign that you've actually been weighing up the evidence as you've been presenting it, and letting it influence your thinking. Of course, if you've followed my advice and written a plan, laying out the arguments pro and contra the thesis of your essay title, you probably already know what you think. But your reader doesn't. So take them on an interesting journey that considers the antithesis before you offer your final synthesis in favour of one side or the other (or perhaps a little of both).

As well as being a good way of generating twice as many ideas; as well as giving your essay a natural, paragraph-by-paragraph, yes-but-no-but-then-again-maybe kind of STRUCTURE and DRIVE; and as well as making you seem fair-minded, as if you haven't made up your mind at paragraph one and are just filling up the pages so you can get to the word count you think you need – on top of all that, and even more important, is the fact that fully considering both sides of an argument is the best and only way of working out for yourself what you REALLY think about a difficult problem.

Fill up your tank

Winston Churchill said:

> It is a good thing for an uneducated man to read books of quotations. *Bartlett's Familiar Quotations* is an admirable work, and I studied it intently. The quotations when engraved upon the memory give you good thoughts. They also make you anxious to read the authors and look for more.

I remember coming across this quotation 20 years ago, in (of course) a book of quotations I had eagerly finagled from some Book of the Month Club's introductory offer, and feeling rather deflated. Owning *The Oxford Dictionary of Quotations*, according to Churchill, made me 'uneducated' – the very thing I thought this book (and a degree from Oxford) would cure. It's only recently I realised that Churchill – who didn't excel at Harrow and left at 18 for Sandhurst and the Army, instead of university – probably didn't regard himself as 'educated' either. This self-perceived lack was probably what drove him, while stationed with his regiment in India, to order from home case after case of great books that he then devoured. Despite his expensive early education, I'd argue he was one of the great autodidacts (= someone self-taught) of the 20th century.

Now, I'm no Churchill, and I did go to university, but I'm

certain I've learned more in the nearly 20 years since I left it than I did in my first 20, most of which were spent in formal education.

> Think of things to say, then say them out loud. You're Churchill. Write them down. You're Shakespeare.

I love this quote, and though I consider myself a tolerably deft Googler, I've been unable to find the source. It reminds me that every great thought, speech and book ever thought or declaimed or written started as a tiny spark in someone's head, and that greatness in most fields of human endeavour is largely just a matter of having brilliant ideas, and following through on them. But those brilliant ideas don't come out of a vacuum. So fill up your tank.

Disagreeing with other people

If you want to learn how to write essays, the best thing you can do is read essays, ideally by the greatest practitioners of the form (you're terribly kind, but I'm not referring to myself here). You can find them everywhere. My favourite essayist around today, by far, is Anthony Daniels, who uses the pen name Theodore Dalrymple. He is wonderful, and you can find a huge tranche of his work at a website run by one of his many fans, called *The Sceptical Doctor* (see previous chapter on 'what to read').

Daniels is a somewhat ill-tempered but humourous retired GP and prison psychiatrist who has practised medicine on at least three continents. His politics are right wing, the opposite of mine, and that's one of the reasons he is indispensable to me. Because when I read him, I feel like I'm seeing the world with binocular vision, rather than the one-eyed view my own political outlook condemns me to. He is another autodidact, extraordinarily widely read (not the same as 'well-read', which is a term akin to 'educated' that seems to snobbishly suggest there are 'right' and 'wrong' books and magazines to read), and writes entertainingly on myriad subjects.

Perhaps his chief concern, though, is the social underclass that he believes the generous welfare system in Western countries has created, by removing the need to work for millions of people if they choose not to, and thereby extinguishing meaning from their lives, with a raft of negative consequences, not just for them, but for the life of these rich nations. Unlike most people on the right wing, Daniels speaks with authority on the subject, because he spent decades treating these people in prisons and in his medical practice in a poor part of Birmingham.

In this he seems to subscribe to 'The Samaritan's Dilemma', a term coined by the American Nobel-winning economist, James Buchanan.

Recent writing about Buchanan has unearthed evidence

that his libertarian beliefs (that taxation is basically theft, and the state should be as small as possible, except for the military, which most libertarians still love) were founded on his secret racist and segregationist attitudes about education. He thought that teaching black and white children together – which was one result of the Civil Rights Movement in the 1960s led by people like Martin Luther King – was wrong.

Now, I happen to disagree strongly with Buchanan's view of educational segregation. 'Separate but equal', which was the policy before the 1960s that Buchanan wanted to return to, can never mean equality, because one side always has more power and money. This is roughly how I feel about the different but comparable divide – along the lines of class rather than race – between private and state education, which has existed in the United Kingdom for centuries. I don't like it.

But I also know that taking on someone's opposing viewpoint, and considering its strengths, is a worthwhile and meaningful thing for me to do – because, if I don't challenge my own views by subjecting them to an opposing one, then I'm not really thinking in any meaningful sense. So I try to read newspapers and magazines that I disagree with. Every so often, they change my mind. And more often, they make me think harder about what I actually think.

I read *The Guardian*, 'The World's leading Liberal Voice', (i.e. left wing), every day, in which Marina Hyde and Barney Ronay are always funny, savage and truthful. I skim *The*

Telegraph (right wing), though there's a semi-porous pay wall, as with *The Economist* (right), *The Spectator* (right), *The New Statesman* (left), *The London Review of Books* (left) and *The New York Review of Books* (left) – but these last two are particularly superb, and there are decades of longer essays online, mostly free. The generally left-leaning American websites Salon, Slate, The Atlantic and The Baffler are also free.

The opposite of Theodore Dalrymple is Laurie Penny, who is a young (well, younger than me) left-wing journalist whom I read and usually either agree or disagree with quite strongly. Either way, she always makes me think. Other essay writers I enjoy, in no particular order, are: Isaiah Berlin, Michel de Montaigne, Zadie Smith, Mark Fisher, Nina Power, George Orwell, Bertrand Russell, Jordan Peterson and Adam Phillips.

Stage two: Aristotle, or persuading other people

In my line of work I read a lot of bad essays. What makes them bad, mostly, is that they contain too many words and not enough thoughts. The fear of the blank page means that most people start writing before they have anything to say. And the form that these empty paragraphs take is usually the same.

The appeal of PEE and PEA

Point Evidence Evaluation, or Point Evidence Analysis. PEE or PEA. They mean the same thing. And they're how most people are taught to write essays. There's nothing wrong with PEE/PEA. It's good to make points. It's important to support those points with evidence – how else are you going to make people believe you? And it's also a fine thing for essayists to evaluate or analyse that evidence – it really just means that you're thinking about what you've just said, which is obviously important. Essays should contain as much thinking as possible.

But I still don't really like PEE/PEA as a template for essays – or paragraphs, because good paragraphs should contain more than one point or piece of evidence or evaluation/analysis of said evidence. The problem with PEE/PEA is that you tend to get a lot of three sentence paragraphs like this one:

> War is bad. 80 million people died in the Second World War. People dying is bad, therefore war is bad.

Obviously I don't disagree with this person's evaluation/analysis. War is bad. And I don't disagree with the general idea of supporting your points with evidence, nor with the notion that it's a good idea to evaluate/analyse your evidence once you've cited it. But I can't help feeling that the person who wrote the paragraph above might have had some more interesting thoughts if they'd spent more time considering the subject more widely, instead of taking the PEE/PEA template and simply plugging the most basic point and evidence and evaluation/analysis into it in order to get three sentences in order to get to the next paragraph. Paragraphs are allowed to contain more than three sentences. This one does. Sometimes a thought can't be contained in a small vessel, and needs to be aerated, like a fine wine, in a larger one.

Also, don't just tell me. Persuade me. But how do you persuade me? I'm glad you asked. It just so happens that someone has thought of that before. His name was Aristotle, and he lived in Athens in the fourth century BC, where he studied under Plato, before coming up with a few ideas of his own.

'ELP!

Aristotle thought there were three ways of persuading someone of the rightness of your arguments. He called them ethos, logos and pathos. Let's have some definitions.

Ethos is where we get the term ethics from – which means acting properly, acting morally. But really ethos is about who the speaker is more generally. Really it's asking the person trying to persuade their reader of something: who are you to tell me what's what? By what authority are you making your argument? Which is a tall order when you're someone with no real professional qualifications to tell anyone what's what. Which is why you'll want to borrow other people's ethos, people who are better qualified to say what's what. Have you noticed how many famous people's opinions I've cited – even better, directly quoted – so far in this book? That's because I want to borrow their ethos to bolster my arguments, to persuade you I'm right. You might not listen to me, but you'll definitely listen to Einstein or Aristotle (now you've heard of him) or Winston Churchill – right? What I've given you here are Aristotle's three elements of rhetoric – which basically means 'persuasive language' – in the original Ancient Greek, which I'm currently translating for you. Why am I doing that? I could easily have said something like 'character' or 'authority' instead of messing around with words like 'ethos'. Because I want you to know that I can read Ancient Greek. Why do I want you to know that? Because it gives me extra ethos to be able to translate the word 'ethos' for you. That's why. It makes me sound like I know what I'm talking about. Which allows me to persuade you more effectively. Ethos.

Logos is easier to define, and easier to remember. It means logic, basically. Facts and figures. Or evidence, if we're still bound by the tyranny of PEE/PEA. But beware. Arguments aren't won by facts alone. In fact, irrational creatures that we are, logos is often the least important of Aristotle's three elements of rhetoric in winning an argument. That doesn't mean you shouldn't offer your reader a relevant, compelling fact in every paragraph you write. You should – you must. It just means that there's more to persuading your reader than simply presenting them with information.

Pathos is an odd one. Pathos means passion or suffering, or emotion. You'd think it had no place in a proper essay, one arguing for and against the truth of a concrete proposal. But it's perhaps the most important of the three. Using pathos to make your case means making your reader feel the truth of what you're saying. As I've already said – but the point bears repeating, as do all important points that we might prefer to ignore – we're not entirely rational creatures. When we make decisions, our feelings play a big role – at least as big a role as our understanding of the facts.

Here's an example. Every British military expedition into a foreign land for the past 25 years has stressed the importance of 'winning the hearts and minds' of the people whose lands they're invading or occupying, or safeguarding. Did you notice that 'safeguarding' sounds better than the other two? The tone of the language you use in your essay is an important aspect of using pathos effectively. If you're arguing in favour of a military expedition, you'll call it something like 'safeguarding', or 'liberating'. Palestine was for many years called a 'British Protectorate', which sounds better than 'colony' or 'military annexe'. If you're arguing against a military expedition, you'll call it an 'invasion' or an 'occupation' or a 'war of aggression'.

'Hearts and minds', then – notice that it's hearts first, then minds. You *first* have to win your reader's trust to *then* persuade them with your superior logical arguments. You do this with Pathos, or not at all. And isn't it the case that, despite we humans regarding ourselves as paragons of reason, we only reach for logic as a tool to justify our emotional gut reactions? Logic is, for most people, a tool to win an argument; the truth is a mere by-product of this process.

Rhetoric and its absence

The problem with rhetoric – defined as 'the effective use of language', remember? – is that if someone notices you're using it to persuade them, then it's immediately less effective. No one likes to feel like they're being manipulated, do they?

That was a rhetorical question, by the way – a very useful rhetorical technique, on which more later. My point is that I just manipulated you into agreeing with me – with that ordinary-sounding, but rather insistent '… do they?' at the end of the last paragraph. Hopefully I did it without you noticing I was doing it.

By the way, beware of people who ask you a series of questions to which the answer is obviously yes ('Can you speak English?' 'Is the sky blue?'), because they're probably about to ask you a question to which your answer might ordinarily be no ('Can you spare some time to talk about disadvantaged cats?').

Okay. So. Hold on to your hats. You might want to sit down for this. Actually, the most effective form of rhetoric – of persuasion – is plain speaking, which is the absence of rhetoric, or at least the apparent absence of it. After all, what's more effective than telling someone exactly what you think in as few and as simple words as possible? (Rhetorical question there.) It's harder than it sounds – I've worked quite hard to do it myself in this chapter, and I can still sense some of you switching off when I get too wordy. But straightforward language, whether real or fake, builds trust.

Ars est celare artem. 'Art means concealing your art', as the Roman poet Ovid said. The most effective rhetorical technique is the art of plain speaking, which means using simple (but persuasive) language in such a subtle way that your audience doesn't notice that they're being persuaded. This is why the traditional opening to a public speech is 'Unaccustomed as I am to public speaking…'. It's a way of telling your audience that you're not going to bamboozle them with fancy words and sentence structures; you're just going to tell them the plain, unvarnished truth.

Oliver Cromwell instructed his portrait painter to depict him 'warts and all', contrary to the traditional habit of painting kings in as flattering a way as possible. But this story about

Cromwell's portrait is much more famous than the portrait itself, and the story is much more flattering than any picture could be, in terms of what it suggests about Cromwell's character. Because it suggests that he cared more about the truth than about just looking good (though, of course, this makes him look good – do you see now how powerful this 'plain-speaking' can be when used properly?).

All of which is to say that, when you're choosing fancy language to persuade your audience you're right, don't overdo it. A little goes a long way.

Rhetorical questions

Look at the title every time you start a new paragraph. It's okay to deviate from this, but only if you know and say why you're deviating. Basically, always ATQ – Answer The Question – because if you're not focused on that, then you're wasting your time, as well as (much more importantly) your reader's.

It's hard, though, when you're having a conversation with someone else, to keep the discussion on a subject you know something about. In an essay – when you're having a conversation with yourself – it's not so hard, though, because you're driving both arguments. And you can use rhetorical questions to get your essay back on track, onto the question you want to answer. What's a rhetorical question? That was a rhetorical question. What is their purpose? (That was another one right there.)

If there's a point you badly want to make that will help your reader understand your wider argument, you can just ask yourself the question, and then answer it. What happens if you ask too many rhetorical questions in a row? (Well spotted...) Your reader probably assumes you've lost your train of thought, and waits for you to start a new argument in a new paragraph.

Over to you

Time for you to do some work. I want you to analyse three paragraphs from my website to see ethos, logos and pathos in action. Now, the purpose of my website is to persuade you that I'm an absolutely marvellous tutor, at whom you should throw all your money because I'll turn you (or your child) into a genius. It doesn't spend any time doing what a balanced essay should do, which is to consider the contrary argument – in this case, the argument that I'm an idiot and a charlatan who will take your money and fill your brain with nonsense. (Hopefully I haven't given you too much evidence to support that counterargument, in any case.)

All you have to do is mark an E, an L or a P next to each of these three paragraphs, depending on which of the three techniques you think I'm using.

1. I studied at Winchester College and Oxford University, and have tutored hundreds of children for thousands of hours over the past 15 years. The writer William Morris said that you should 'Have nothing in your house that you do not know to be useful, or believe to be beautiful', and I think the same is true of education – that its purpose is to fill our heads with things we find useful, or beautiful, or hopefully both.

2. Around 50% of my scholarship students have been successful in their applications to Winchester, Eton and Westminster, the three schools which set the most demanding exams. The usual success rate at these exams is more like 25%. So my help makes a measurable difference.

3. I have tutored the children of billionaires and the children of refugees. Some of my students attend the best, most expensive schools in London, and don't really need my help: they're surrounded by highly educated experts who make it almost impossible for them to fail. And some of my students, from poorer backgrounds, I teach for 1% of my usual fee. I do this because I grew up poor myself and I understand how life-changing it can be to go to an extraordinary school. Some of my students will do better than others, and I can usually predict who will succeed quite easily. But the thing that marks them out for success isn't the wealth or the poverty of their backgrounds. It's whether or not they believe in Disinterested Learning, which is to say – are they learning disinterestedly, for the sheer love of it; or are they studying simply to pass their exams? When I meet a student who loves their subject, when I can see they want to learn, even with no grades or praise or scholarships to be won – then I know that their future is bright, whatever their past was like.

1. This is using ethos – I'm asserting my own authority/expertise in the area to be argued and, where necessary, citing other authorities/experts – in this case, William Morris.

2. Here's logos – or logic – which is using a reasoned argument to persuade my reader I'm right, which means citing relevant facts to support the reasoned argument that 'my help makes a difference'.

3. And this is pathos – notice that I'm not making a fact-based argument, or using my own or anyone's else's authority to make a point. Instead, I'm trying to excite your emotions by contrasting rich and poor, privileged and deprived – and then saying that this doesn't matter, that there's something about education that can erase those deep and terrible divides, and that it's available to everyone if they can find within themselves this universal quality of curiosity. I've presented you with division and unfairness and pain, and then replaced it with hope and a conception of humanity in which we're all the same and can all raise ourselves up, however humble our beginnings. There's also a bit of ethos there, given I make myself sound like a nice guy for working with underprivileged children. But this is nearly all pathos – you feel these words, rather than think about them.

So, logos, ethos and pathos, then – they're three different tools to be used in different proportions depending on:

- What you're arguing about (there's room for emotion if you're talking about starting a war; less so if you're shouting about what the shortest route to the M25 is).
- Whom you're arguing with (examiners like logos, with quotes or examples supporting that logic; toddlers respond better to ethos – Are you going to be good? – and pathos – Let's play a fun game where we pick up all our toys!).
- Who you are (you don't want to lean too much on ethos if you're 13 and not a professor of anything, though you can of course get round that by quoting actual experts to support your points. Notice how many famous people I quote in the course of this book to bolster my own arguments).

Ethos and style

Ethos is about more than just 'Who are you to be telling me this?', or naming a respected authority whose power you borrow by quoting their expert words to support your own. On a word-by-word level, ethos means using precise and sometimes technical terminology, in exactly the right way to show you understand the exact meanings of those terms.

With language, precision is important; pomposity, pretension, periphrasis, plagiarism and sesquipedalianism are to be avoided at all costs – as this sentence demonstrates – because it makes you sound like you're trying too hard, which makes you sound like you're using long words to cover up the fact that you don't really know what you're talking about. If you must use them, long words work best in short sentences, maybe compared with another long word to show you understand the difference between the two, or at least in a sentence that shows you actually understand what it means.

But if you think you might be overdoing it with the long words, you probably are. As Mark Twain said, 'Don't use a five-dollar word when a 50-cent word will do'. Simplicity is best. Twain again: 'When you catch an adjective, kill it'. Rookie writers often use adjectives to make their arguments for them, or just to embroider their sentences.

And watch out for sentences that over-equivocate or over-explain, or just plain over-run. If an idea needs two sentences, give it two. And if you change your mind mid-sentence, you haven't thought it through enough. Cross it out, put your pen down and work out what you really think. Because it's unethical to try to persuade your reader of something if you don't yet believe it yourself. It's like you're selling someone a car you know will break down. Or a financial product you know will make them poorer rather than richer.

Ethos and ethics

I know I quote a lot of famous men and women – mainly men I'm afraid, which is partly because I'm a man, and partly because through history more men have had the opportunity to make themselves heard. But quoting someone famous isn't the end of the conversation – no human, however celebrated today, has ever got through a whole life without doing or saying a fair few foolish or wrongheaded things.

Some of the greatest minds of today will seem, with the benefit of 1000 or 100 or even ten years' hindsight, like selfish, shortsighted idiots. Most, of course, will be completely forgotten. This is not only inevitable, but necessary. This is why we read old books. It's not because they were right about everything. It's to have a conversation with the past, retrieving old authorities to hold their supposed wisdom up to the light of all the new knowledge, that was unavailable to them then, but that we have now. Is it still true? Or is it nonsense?

As we've seen, ethos means ethics, really – they come from the same Greek word – and both of those things depend on empathy. How do you think about the world? How do you think about other people? What sort of person are you?

In a public debate on a particular yes/no question, the audience are asked before the debate whether they are for or against the proposition to be debated, and then asked again afterwards. The winning side is judged not to be the side that ends up with the most votes in the second vote, but the side that persuaded the most people to change their minds. In an essay, both sides are played by you. But just as importantly, so is your reader. Your reader, really, is your conscience and you must convince them too.

Capital punishment

Okay, so here's another essay plan. As I've said, a good essay looks like a tennis match, because you're setting up two great players to bash balls back and forth, against each other, with the final judgement uncertain until the end. There should be conflict until the very final paragraph.

The way I would arrange all these points – these paragraphs – is by jumping from one side of the argument to the other. I've numbered them for you to show the ideal running order. Trust me: you'll look dynamic, and your reader will stay engaged. Also, notice how the points opposite each other – 1 versus 2, 3 vs 4, and 5 vs 6 – are basically mirror images. I had three ideas, and then I thought the opposite and turned those three points into six. (I couldn't find an opposite for point 7, which is pretty much why that's my decisive and final point.)

Final thought, and the most important one: I've put what I believe are the two strongest points of the seven in bold. Try to open with your second best point, then close with your best. Why? It's a basic rule of showbusiness: grab their attention, then leave them wanting more.

AMERICA SHOULD ABOLISH CAPITAL PUNISHMENT

Abolish (pro)	Retain (contra)
1. **Europe – where America got most of its good ideas, like democracy, and the rule of law, and the separation of church and state, and capitalism – doesn't execute criminals – ETHOS**	2. Can poor states really afford to keep dangerous people – who this way will never contribute anything to society – alive for the rest of their lives? Prisons are expensive – LOGOS
3. Death penalty doesn't work as a deterrent to murder – America has the highest murder rate in the Western World – LOGOS	4. Death penalty is the ultimate deterrent despite what anyone says – LOGOS
5. 'Thou shalt not kill' – ETHOS	6. 'An eye for an eye, a tooth for a tooth' – ETHOS
7. **Mistakes can be made in murder trials which can't be repaired: prisoners can be compensated for wrongful imprisonment; but if the executed person was innocent, execution is terribly final – PATHOS**	

The death penalty is a state-by-state decision, with 31 of 50 of US states currently executing prisoners. Interestingly, it's only in the past 30 years that the campaign against the death penalty has had any success in shifting public opinion: support for capital punishment was at 80% nationwide in 1994 and has fallen to 49% as of 2016. Much of this change is due to former death-row convicts – men who had been sentenced to death but were then freed because their convictions were found to be false – speaking at campaign events, explaining that they would be dead today if it weren't for certain mistakes or oversights coming to light.

> Many that live deserve death. And some that die deserve life. Can you give it to them? Then do not be too eager to deal out death in judgment. For even the very wise cannot see all ends.
> *JRR Tolkien, The Fellowship of the Ring*

So it's not always logical arguments about what does and doesn't work (aka logos), or arguments from the authority of respected sources (ethos), that change people's minds. Sometimes it's the emotional shock of seeing someone telling their story, someone who would be dead today but for a wrongful justice being overturned, that wins an argument. In other words, pathos works. You should always argue for what you feel in your heart is right. Ethos, logos and pathos – and rhetoric more generally – are simply tools for doing so.

Stage three: five types of paragraph

In my opinion, there are five types of paragraph in an essay that's trying to answer a difficult question:

1. Yes (aka pro, agreeing with question's proposition, giving details and reasons and citing authorities)
2. No (aka contra, disagreeing with the question's proposition)
3. Attack the language of the question
4. Attack the assumptions of the question
5. Have brilliant ideas

1 and 2: yes and no, pro and contra

Try thinking the opposite, as I've said. But don't insist on finding an equal number of pros and cons for every essay. There are a lot of bad ideas in the world. That's what committees are for, what arguments are for – to stop bad ideas becoming bad laws, or bad policies or bad movies. And anyway, you probably already know in your gut which side you're going to end up arguing on. Just show me you've thought about the arguments the other side would make, too.

Also, this binary yes/no stuff can be wearying. And maybe there are more than two sides to every argument. Maybe the yes/no structure is a straitjacket that prevents creative thinking and brilliant solutions. Hegel thought two opposite ideas (thesis and antithesis, remember?) – say capitalism and communism – collided and fought and formed a new consensus (synthesis), which I suppose would be whatever we've got now. And that then a new opposite idea to that would arise and the whole thing would play out again.

But what's the next big opposing idea of how to run the world, that's going to take on the current synthesis (which most people call neoliberal capitalism)? What's the next antithesis? Is it islamo-fascism? Anti-globalisation neo-nationalism? Neither of those ideas seems particularly great. They aren't going to solve any of the major problems we face today – global warming, economic inequality, nuclear war. Is it worth spending the next century debating the arguments pro and contra one of these two ideas, while the world gets hotter and angrier and more dangerous?

So don't play devil's advocate just for the hell of it. You need to be honest about where you feel the answer truly lies. It's just that the act of examining the opposite argument, tends to temper – which means to strengthen steel with extreme heat – one's initial arguments.

And if it turns out, having studied both sides of the argument, that your first, gut response was wrong, well, you've got something more out of this than a few well-turned paragraphs. You've changed your own mind by laying out and examining your prejudices. And that's a habit you now have in common with every other intelligent person in the world.

3: attack the language of the question

I know I mentioned at the very start that it's traditional to begin an essay by defining your terms as you intend to use them – but actually it can be more interesting, more dynamic, and more conflicting to ask the same question midway through. Especially if you've run out of yes/no paragraph ideas.

But it's much more than that. Define your terms, because the words you choose to make your arguments matter. In 1940 the communist British historian Christopher Hill wrote a book that reassessed the meaning of the English Civil War of 300 years earlier, which saw the overthrow of the aristocracy (Cavaliers) and the execution of Charles I by the middle classes (Roundheads) led by Oliver Cromwell, who abolished the monarchy and established England as a republic. Then Cromwell died and Charles's son was crowned Charles II, re-establishing the English monarchy, which is why we still have a queen today, although as a result of the Civil War her power is now limited and parliament is sovereign.

But Hill didn't call his book *The English Civil War*. He called it *The English Revolution, 1640*. Why? Why not just use the same term everyone else uses to describe that conflict? Was he deliberately being difficult? And what's the difference between a civil war and a revolution, anyway? Well, he was being difficult, but with a purpose. England had had several civil wars before – which saw two groups of landowning aristocrats compete for the throne – but never a revolution; nor had any other country in the world. The word 'revolution' has a very specific meaning, and Hill used the word deliberately to underline the central thesis of his book. A revolution is a class war, in which a lower social group achieves class consciousness and attempts to overthrow the rule of a higher social group in order to rule in its place. Hill was arguing that England was the first country where the middle class had become powerful enough and educated enough to attempt this, and that the English Civil War should more correctly be called *The English Revolution*.

Over a century after the English revolution (Charles I was executed in 1649) came the American (1776), French (1789), Chinese (1911) and Russian (1917) revolutions, which were more successful than the English in permanently abolishing their monarchies (or the rule of a foreign monarchy in America's case). These nations are all republics, whereas Britain is still a monarchy, because their revolutions succeeded where ours failed. Christopher Hill – a communist, remember, and therefore opposed to all monarchies – uses the word 'revolution' to remind us of that failure.

History tells the story of how our country got where we are today. So the convention whereby historians – still to this day, despite Hill's attempt to rebrand it – call the events of 1642–1651 a 'civil war' rather than a 'revolution' is a deeply conservative one. It uses language to conceal the truth from the English people of today, the truth of what really happened in those ten years: that the English – having together determined that they had the right to choose how, and by whom they should be governed – rose up together against tyranny and killed their king.

The reason for the English revolution's official designation by the British establishment as a mere 'civil war', Hill suggests, is to deny that any such revolutionary class struggle ever happened – presumably for fear that it might happen again. Likewise, the success of Cromwell's New Model Army in defeating Royalist ground forces in that 'civil war' has led to the domination of the British Army's upper ranks by aristocrats of varying ability. It's also why most British military disasters have happened to the Army, rather than the 'senior service' – the navy – or the newer Royal Air Force. Why? Because in any country, including Britain, only the army has the ability to seize power from a civilian government: ships and planes only get you so far. All of the world's military dictators are former army officers – generals, not admirals or air commodores.

So, to prevent the possibility of an army *coup d'etat*, the British monarchy has traditionally promoted only their fellow aristocrats to the highest ranks of the British army – rather than in the other two services, where promotion is based on merit. Because aristocratic generals can be relied upon to support the monarchy – a middle- or working-class revolution would not be in their interests. In the past this has meant that there were always a few incompetent toffs in charge of the troops, which led to disasters like the Charge of the Light Brigade during the Crimean War, or the Gallipoli Landings during the First World War (or indeed any number of battles in that war).

And while we're on the subject of names and their hidden meanings – what name do you think Prince Charles will take when he becomes king? If you said Charles III, you're probably wrong. Why? Historically, most English/British monarchs have reigned under their given first name. So why do many authorities think he'll reign under another name? Because names, and the associations they have, matter. If you skip back to the start of this section, you'll notice that Charles I and II didn't have very successful reigns: Charles II was the first powerless King of England; his father Charles I was the first headless one.

The wonderful website 'Wait But Why' did an analysis of the popularity of baby names over the 20th century, and noticed a sudden but predictable drop, after 1945, of parents calling their sons Adolf. A steep drop, then, but not to zero: clearly some people thought it was good enough for their little darling. I bet that kid had a hard time in the playground. As I said, names matter.

So analyse why other people use the words they do. Quite possibly they're hiding something, even if they don't know it. And be precise in the words you use – you may want to explain what you understand by the technical terms you use, and why you chose them.

4: attack the assumptions of the question

There was a question on an Eton Scholarship paper in 2012 that I'm going to bully a bit, for the sake of an example, and for my amusement:

> Wars are begun more due to fear than anger.
> How far do you agree with this statement?

I hope you never forget that you have the option to really go after the question itself, to attack either the terms in which it is asked (as in the above section), or to attack the underlying premise and the assumptions it makes. That is what I would be tempted to do here. Because who really starts wars? Not the people, not even in a democracy; they are brought along for the ride emotionally by propaganda, but only after the decision has been made by a leader or a tiny elite. And those decisions are usually made by logic and calculation and strategic self-interest.

'War is the continuation of policy with other means', as the German general Carl von Clausewitz said, so the two resemble each other in theory if not in practice. The three main Western theories of foreign policy are – in descending order of idealism – Utopian ('wouldn't it be nice if...'); Grotian (pragmatism and idealism balanced); and Machiavellian ('the ends justify the means' – i.e. anything goes). None of these theories has much room for emotion, although in practice it creeps in, because everyone involved is a human being.

My point is this. The way the question is framed – 'Wars are begun more due to fear than anger' – suggests the person asking it assumes all wars are started as an expression of a nation's will. Clearly, this is false on two levels: the decision to go to war is not made by the nation as a whole and is not made on the basis of emotion. This is also the kind of lie that the tiny elite deciding to start those wars like to have the rest of the nation's people believe. Indeed, they work very hard to make those people believe that lie, especially those who will be fighting and dying in those wars. So it's an assumption that's well worth attacking.

5: have brilliant ideas

I always like to ask my students what they're up to at school, partly because I'm interested in my students, but mainly because I want to steal the ideas that their teachers have taught them and then pass them off as my own. So when one of my students told me his teacher had just given them a class on how to write essays, I was all ears. This teacher had one main idea, and it was this: have brilliant ideas.

It seems so simple now, doesn't it? People love brilliant

ideas – just put a few brilliant ideas down on paper and you're golden. Happy days.

I'm not being sarcastic – it really is the best advice for writing essays that I've ever heard and it's the only advice, out of everything I've told you so far, that I'd insist you heed. Because it should always be in the back of your mind, the possibility that you're going to come up with something brilliant. Where you put your brilliant idea, how it fits into the structure of your essay, whether you open or close with it – these are all of secondary importance.

The great Dutch footballer and manager Johan Cruyff, who trained Pep Guardiola at Barcelona, could play in any position on the field. A star player is a star player, wherever you put them. And, while structure is important, the most important thing in any essay is brilliant ideas. So, how do you have them? Well, it's hard. Especially if you have a time limit. Here's what John Cleese, a member of Monty Python,[18] and therefore one of the funniest people this island has produced, says about having brilliant ideas:

> This is the extraordinary thing about creativity: if just you keep your mind resting against the subject in a friendly but persistent way, sooner or later you will get a reward from your unconscious.

[18] Who made *The Life of Brian* and *The Holy Grail*, two of the funniest films ever, and still funny 40 years on which is very rare.

If I can add anything to Cleese's advice, vis-à-vis your essay plan (we're still planning, remember – you're unlikely to come up with your world-shaking idea if you're bogged down with worrying about where the commas go), it's simply this. Try to think about how apparently unrelated things might be connected.

Occam's Razor is a wonderful thing: it's William of Occam's theory that the most simple and obvious explanation for anything is usually the correct one, and that complicated additional explanations should therefore be cut away, with his metaphorical Razor (see chapter seven for examples of this). But this theory isn't always right, because (ask any historian) complex events often have complex causes – and anyway, what's obvious to one person isn't obvious to another.

So, when you're thinking creatively, try to connect things that aren't obviously connected. You might come up with something interesting. And also, whomever you're writing this essay for, you won't go too far wrong if you can manage to thrill them with your intellectual imagination. Here are two examples of ideas I find particularly thrilling.

Brilliant idea number one: zinc. In 1999, the British Foreign Office charged the philosopher Edward De Bono with resolving conflict in the Middle East, which has been going on for at least 100 years. It is too complicated to explain here, but involves oil, Islam, colonialism by Western countries including the US, the secret Sykes-Picot Treaty between

Britain and France in 1916, and the creation of the state of Israel in 1948.

De Bono's brilliant idea was this. The people in the Middle East largely eat unleavened flatbread, which means bread made without yeast – yeast is the micro-organism used in Western countries to make bread rise into the fluffy loaves you probably think of when I mention the word bread. Now, yeast does more than just make loaves rise in the oven. It contains large amounts of zinc, which among other things is important in the proper functioning of the brain. Lack of zinc makes people more irritable, quicker to anger. So De Bono's suggestion was this: we should donate Marmite, which is a sandwich spread containing large amounts of zinc, to Middle Eastern countries, in the hope that it would lead to less anger in these countries, and thereby to a negotiated peace.

It didn't work. Since De Bono's idea, there have been several wars in the Middle East and millions have died. In De Bono's defence, some of those wars involved Western countries. In 2003, Iraq was invaded and occupied by the US and Britain, countries that already eat bread made with yeast, who should know better according to this thinking, which suggests De Bono's idea was too simplistic – that wars don't happen just because those countries' people might feel a bit more angry on average.

But let's look at how De Bono came up with that idea.

We can only guess at his thought processes, of course, but let's look at the categories he made links between with this brilliant idea. He started with a political problem and thought about it in quite different terms. A country's politics is rooted in its culture, you might say. And part of a country's culture – an especially important part in a country at war, because as the French General Napoleon said, 'an army marches on its stomach' – is the kind of food its people eat. From politics to culture to food – it seems obvious when you put it that way.

Brilliant idea number two: lead. Another brilliant idea along these lines, around the same time but on a much larger scale, does seem to have worked. It was shown in the 1970s that lead, which in those days was present in petrol, in paint and in plumbing, has a negative effect on children's brain development, making them less intelligent and more likely to be violent. Indeed, the Latin word *plumbum* gives us the chemical abbreviation Pb, and more importantly the English word 'plumbing' – for centuries, pipes carrying drinking water have been made of lead.

One theory about the fall of the Roman Empire 1600 years ago is that they had all gone mad from drinking lead-contaminated water. Today, in any case, banning the use of lead in petrol, which took decades of activism all over the world, has led to a dramatic drop in violent crime globally. The United Nations estimated the ban led to 1.2 million fewer premature deaths and 58 million fewer crimes.

Imagine you're the person who had that brilliant idea. You've just saved a million lives, and improved tens of millions.

Not all your ideas will work as you hope. Probably most of them won't. But some of them will.

Humanity needs brilliant ideas. It always has, since fire and tools and language. The person who will solve climate change has probably already been born. Let's hope they have. If they haven't, it's probably too late.

So have brilliant ideas. We're counting on you.

THIRD QUESTION

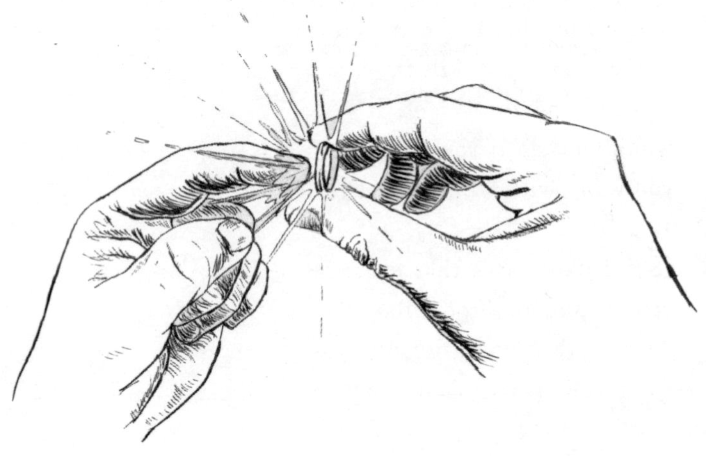

THE RING OF GYGES

Plato tells the story of a shepherd, Gyges, who finds a magic ring that can make him invisible. Gyges uses it to seduce the queen, kill the king, marry her and rule in his place. Good for Gyges. It's a common question – what would you do if you were invisible? You can do anything you want, without being caught. What would you do?

JRR Tolkien asks that question of Bilbo Baggins in *The Hobbit* and of Frodo Baggins in *The Lord of the Rings.* They both spend a lot of time in possession of the One Ring, which gives them the power of invisibility. Why does neither of them end up rich, or powerful? If *you* had such a ring,

what would you do?

Would you seek money, or power? And, just as importantly,

what would you not do?

5

HOW TO TELL A STORY

I. Action, dialogue, description

In *On Writing*, Stephen King's brief and brilliant writing guide/autobiography, he says there are only three kinds of sentence:

Action;
Dialogue; and
Description.

Most of my students, when I ask them to write a story, write too many sentences of the first kind, and not enough of the third. Which is understandable, because action is what tells the story. But description (and to an extent dialogue) is what makes a story feel real to your reader, and if it doesn't feel real, then why read on?

Let's start with action.

'Tell the truth, but tell it slant'

In storytelling, as in life, we should be guided by Mark Twain's reminder that 'If you always tell the truth, you don't have to remember anything.' It's been shown that someone fabricating a story uses half the vocabulary and a fraction of the detail, imagery and insight that a more reliable reporter employs. 'Stretchers' of the truth are acceptable, as Twain's hero Huckleberry Finn allows, but any lie is best hidden between two truths. You should ground every story, however fantastical its details, in a recent vivid experience, because the sensory and emotional content will feel 50 times more *real* if the author has lived through it himself.

A lie is best hidden between two truths

Always bear in mind that, however outlandish the setting and the characters in your story, it's going to be read by humans. These humans will have experienced more or less the same kind of world that you've experienced, in much the same way (through their eyes, ears, noses, etc). So you should always try to relate it to what your reader's world is like. It's how you make things that are invented and unreal *really* feel real for your reader. Here's an example.

Growing up, George Lucas was very interested in hot rods. Hot rods were American cars, often slightly crappy ones, in the 1950s and 1960s, that their owners had modified to go faster, often in slightly dangerous ways. It was a big thing back then, an entire youth culture, like surfing or rock music. When he came to make *Star Wars* in 1977, which, remember, was set in a galaxy far, far away, he remembered this obsession, and gave that obsession to Han Solo.

You probably don't remember Han Solo driving a car. Right. But he did have a spaceship, the Millennium Falcon, that he was unreasonably proud of, that he claimed 'made the Kessel Run in less than 12 parsecs', despite basically being a piece of crap with wires hanging out of it, which seemed to spend more time being repaired than flying around in space, and when it did always seemed to break down or get tractor-beamed into Imperial Death Stars. The Millennium Falcon was basically a hot rod, but in space. Lucas took something that was real to him, changed a couple of details, and made it fantastic.

Likewise, no one knows what it's like to be shot by a laser. Probably it feels hot, like burning your hand on a toaster. But hotter. And not many people these days know what it's like to be hit with a sword. But maybe some of you have cut yourselves with a knife while chopping vegetables. I nearly lost a finger-tip that way, and I'll never forget it. Ouch! Now, take a laser, and cross it with a sword, to make a lightsaber. It's still unfamiliar, but you can sort of imagine it. It's like a really, really hot knife.

A big part of George Lucas's genius is there in the Millennium Falcon and the lightsaber, because he took a completely different universe and put familiar things in there, to make us really *feel* what it would be like. That's what you should do in your stories – you should ground them in real life, in what you know, however fantastical the world, in order to bring your reader with you as you describe it.

Make it personal, then change the details

Ian Fleming created Bond, but before that he *actually worked for MI6*. What can you write about with expert knowledge? Think about your audience. People love to learn something new. That's why teachers always set 'What did you do on holiday?'. Because they want to read something interesting. Something true. It doesn't just mean travelling to an interesting country or staying in a seven-star hotel, where I imagine relatively few interesting things happen. It means an unusual situation. People want something they've never had before. Even if it's something fairly boring and mundane to you – it might not be to them.

You don't have to make it completely personal, or autobiographical, just that there should be something of yourself in there somewhere, otherwise it's merely a technical exercise.

Cause and effect

'The king died and then the queen died' are two separate events that happened one after the other. 'The king died and then the queen died *of grief*' has causation, consequence and therefore meaning – the things we look for in a story. (With apologies to EM Forster.)

Matt Parker and Trey Stone, the creators of the long-running satirical cartoon show *South Park*, have one rule about stories. Whenever a writer proposes a story for an episode of the show, they always look for instances of the phrase 'and then'. 'And then', in their view, is fatal to a story, because of what's missing. Causation. *Why* did something happen is at least as important as *what* happened. Just saying 'and then' tells you about chronology, but nothing about the *why* of your story.

Stories exist to show causation. That's why we, as a species, have always needed stories, and probably always will. Because they show us the likely consequences of our actions *without us having to actually take those actions in real life*. Science may have surpassed stories (aka religion) as a way of explaining many aspects of the world, but it hasn't solved love, say, or economics (which is only sort-of a Science), or indeed my field, education.

ADD

In a story, as I've said, there are only three kinds of sentence: action, dialogue and description. You don't have to use them in equal amounts, but if you don't know what to write, you could simply put:

A..

D..

D..

on a blank page, and then write a sentence of action, dialogue and description next to each letter. You've just written a paragraph of your story. Now for the next one.

There are three acts to a story,[19] like Aristotle said, a *beginning*, a *middle* and an *end*, or as the modern American playwright David Mamet explained it:

1. Put your hero in a tree;
2. Throw rocks at her;
3. Get her down again.

Have a go at using this three act model as a template for a short story. You could start by telling it in three paragraphs, each made up of action, dialogue and description (ADD, as above).

Dialogue

Dialogue is even harder than action to make rules about. You don't have to use it at all. If you do, though, you should make

[19] Shakespeare wrote in five acts, but between you and me, the guy didn't have a clue what he was doing.

a habit of eavesdropping on people on public transport and then try to imitate them. The acid test of your dialogue (like all of your writing, but more so) is how it sounds when you read it aloud. The American crime writer Elmore Leonard said you should never use any word other than 'said'[20] after a piece of dialogue, and that's pretty good advice. Finally, though it doesn't relate to dialogue, consider the advice of Leonard's fellow crime writer, Raymond Chandler, about what to do if you can't think of what to write next:

> When in doubt, have a man come through the door with a gun in his hand.

It's a perfect story sentence, containing:

1. Action – storywise, you've just put your hero up a tree, which is where you want him. Your audience ('What does this new guy want and what's he willing to do to get it?') is in suspense – which is where you want them.

2. Description – there's so little of it, no adjectives, and man, door, gun and hand are surely the plainest nouns any writer ever put together in a sentence. But using the plainest words you can – using no style at all – is a style in itself. Maybe even the hardest style to write. No extra fat on your words means you pick just the short, tough ones that say it straight.

---

[20] As I've said earlier...

Description – inside and outside

There are six universal human emotions which it is your job to evoke in your reader through your words, or your hero's troubles: joy, sadness, fear, anger, surprise and disgust.

The American psychologist Paul Ekman found that anyone from any country can recognise these six emotions in anyone else – they are *universal.* So you should use dialogue to express the emotions your characters feel, as much as to convey information (of course, action and description can convey emotion too).

Finally, we each have five senses – so use description to explain to your reader the way the world of your story looks, sounds, feels, smells and tastes.

You can do even more than that, in fact. Synaesthesia is a condition where someone confuses one sense with another ('It smelled late', says one of the narrators of William Faulkner's novel *The Sound and the Fury*). Marcel Proust's multi-novel story *In Search of Lost Time* begins with the narrator tasting a madeleine (a sort of small cake), which is what makes him remember the events of the entire story. Evoking the senses makes a story *feel real.*

'A man who looks like he was born in debt' is how the film writer Ryan Gilbey (he writes for several papers including *The Independent* and the *New Statesman*) described the actor Stephen Rea. What Gilbey did there was to take something external (a face) and turn it into something internal (what it feels like to be in debt your whole life). It's a brilliant trick if you can pull it off, because as readers we're generally more interested in what someone's like on the inside, in what makes them tick – but all we can see, or perceive with our other four senses, is what's on the outside. So if you can find a way to unify the two, you're onto something.

George Orwell said that 'at 50, every man has the face he deserves', which is probably a more famous instance of the same thing – that your character (interior) eventually becomes your face (exterior). Roald Dahl said much the same thing in *The Twits*, as I recall.

But I used the example of Stephen Rea so I could put a picture of him here, and to mention that, while he has usually worked as a character actor, the one major film he had the lead role in was also in my opinion the best thriller of the 1990s – *The Crying Game.*

Make it emotional

After you've given your hero a problem, you need to think about how to make your reader identify with your hero. They shouldn't just understand the hero's problem, they should *feel* it, too. This is expressed in action:

> A huge rotten branch fell on Tony, shattering his knees and pinning him to the ground'

in dialogue:

> 'Aaargh!' he screamed, though no one was there to hear him; no one human, anyway

and in description:

> The forest stretched as far as he could see, which wasn't far, because night was falling, and the temperature was dropping, and the howling of the wolves was getting louder, or perhaps closer.

This wolf paragraph – these three sentences put together – could be the beginning, middle or end of a one paragraph story. It could be a final cliffhanger after he's escaped from a prison gang, or a prelude to battle with wolves, when he's saved by a mysterious man, who then kidnaps him, etc.

The point is to give your reader an experience. Plot/action is only important in that it gives you a way of putting interesting emotions or images into your reader's mind.

I know I've repeated this point ad nauseam elsewhere, but it really matters here: these are suggestions, not rules or even guidelines, really. You can't think of all these rules as you write and you shouldn't – there's no room for the imaginative or the personal if you're just following a checklist. Pick whatever you want and ignore the rest, and even then, you only need to come back to any of this stuff when your well of inspiration runs dry.

Description: I am a camera

Because I love films, and because sight is the most important of our five senses, I think the best way to think about description is to try to picture your story as a movie. This is really useful when you're thinking about *what* to describe – what is going to catch your reader's attention – but also in terms of *how* to describe it. Most obviously, is this a close-up ('streams of sweat ran into her eyes as she fiddled with the detonator'), or a wide shot ('The lone and level sands stretch far away')?

Steven Spielberg is the greatest popular filmmaker of his generation because he makes us *see* his heroes' emotions. There's a shot he puts in almost every film where the hero sees something amazing, or terrifying, or both. But Spielberg doesn't let us see this amazing/terrifying thing yet – he keeps us in suspense, which is another great storytelling technique you should use. (Only tell us what we need to know in that moment; hold the best bits back for the most powerful moments. Suspense is powerful because we're by nature a very curious species.)

But Spielberg isn't just building suspense. What he does before showing us this amazing sight, crucially, is show us the hero's face. And it's the look of wonder, or terror, on our hero's face that primes us, the audience, to feel the same emotion that we can see on his or her face: it makes our own reaction when we finally see what they can see so much stronger. The suspension of the revelation allows us to experience the emotions of the character alongside them, rather than from the outside looking in.

Conclusion: The Ex Libris game

Good writing begins with good reading, and this is particularly true with the ability to mimic the authorial voice of another. All writers begin their careers under the influence of another writer.

TS Eliot said that 'Immature poets imitate; mature poets steal'. You can steal what you like as long as it's just a tiny fragment. Take a character detail rather than a plot and it'll be much less obvious you've pinched something.

But the Ex Libris game – invented, I think, by Oxford Games in 1991 who sell a marvellous edition of it – is about imitation. And you can play it as long as you have a library of, say, a dozen novels, and one other person.

Essentially, you take a piece of paper and fold it into four quarters. Then unfold it. Then you take a novel the other player(s) haven't read, or read over a year ago. In the upper two quadrants of your folded sheet, you write the first sentence of the novel (not the introduction, and not the preface – the first words that appear under the heading Chapter I). You write the first sentence out twice, once in each quadrant.

In one of the two remaining lower quadrants, write the second sentence of the novel. *Then*, in the last of the four remaining quadrants, *write your own alternative second sentence*.

The idea of the exercise is that you look at the first and second sentences of this novel – by Virginia Woolf or George Eliot or Jonathan Franzen or whoever, though classic authors, or at least popular ones, tend to be better – and you take on the authorial voice of a great writer to such an extent that you become them, *for one sentence only*. 'Tonight, Matthew, I'm going to be – Anthony Trollope.'

The idea of the game is that you then show your page to the other player(s), and they have to guess which one is the real second sentence. If they're right, they get a point. If they're wrong, you do.

Small point of order: you can't just reproduce the real second sentence changing one or two words, so I'd suggest this rule: In your fake second sentence, you can't use any words longer than three letters that are also used in the real second sentence. And the other player(s) have to say *why they've chosen this sentence*, too, which means, actually, you're criticising each other's work with the same seriousness that you criticise Swift or Austen or Dickens or Woolf.

Writers fret over first sentences, and the opening of any published book is an example of a piece of prose that has been painstakingly worked on so that it says a great deal with a few words. So you should study openings.

Here are some of my attempts. I'm not going to tell you which ones are real, because you can find out for yourself. Below them are a few openings for you to try writing a second sentence for. They're all pretty famous, so Googling these first sentences will give you the real second ones to compare with your imitations, once you've written them.

The real test, though, is whether you can fool someone else into choosing your imitation second sentence over the real one when they're placed side-by-side.

Option 1

All this happened, more or less. The war parts, anyway, are pretty much true.

Option 2

All this happened, more or less. And if I've told lies, you'll understand that they were told only in the service of the truth.

Option 1

Mother died today. Or maybe yesterday, I don't know.

Option 2

Mother died today. She outlived all her seven children but me, and even that wasn't for want of trying.

Option 1

In my younger and more vulnerable years my father gave me some advice that I've been turning over in my mind ever since. Whenever you feel like criticizing any one, he told me, just remember that all the people in this world haven't had the advantages that you've had.

Option 2

In my younger and more vulnerable years my father gave me some advice that I've been turning over in my mind ever since. Neither a borrower nor a lender be, he told me: wise words, perhaps, but odd ones to hear coming from a banker.

You can easily Google these openings to see if you guessed which was the real one and which was fake. And when you're ready to take on the challenge yourself, try looking up the famous first lines on the next page. Find the sentence that follows them and attempt your own alternative second sentence. Are they good enough to fool an astute reader?

A beginning is a very delicate time.

It was the day my grandmother exploded.

All happy families are alike; each unhappy family is unhappy in its own way.

The sky above the port was the color of television, tuned to a dead channel.

As Gregor Samsa awoke one morning from uneasy dreams he found himself transformed in his bed into a gigantic insect.

....

....

....

'And don't forget,' my father would say, as if he expected me at any moment to up and leave to seek my fortune in the wide world, 'whatever you learn about people, however bad they turn out, each one of them has a heart, and each one of them was once a tiny baby sucking his mother's milk...' [21]

....

....

....

[21] If you're having trouble finding this, it's from Graham Swift's *Waterland*.

THE RING OF GYGES

Answer

Of the two questions asked – What would you do if you were invisible? What would you not do? – the second is much more interesting. The answers to the first are usually bound up in fantasies of power and revenge. We all carry these fantasies inside us, but they can't be realised in our actual lives, and in nearly every case, if we're honest with ourselves, they shouldn't be either.

HG Wells's novel *The Invisible Man* is one answer to the first question, and it's a tragedy, really, because it's the story of a brilliant scientist who discovers the formula for invisibility, tests it successfully on himself, and then finds himself alienated from everyone he knows and loves, and hated and feared by everyone else. They see him as a monster, and so he becomes that monster.

Gyges and Bilbo and Frodo have an advantage that Wells's Invisible Man doesn't: unlike him, they can simply take the invisibility ring off and return to visible normality. The Invisible Man is permanently trapped in his invisibility: he tries, and fails to find an antidote. One of our deepest needs as humans is to be seen, in the metaphorical sense, by others, known by them for who we truly are. Try to imagine how lonely that must be: never to be seen, and therefore never to be loved, by another human being.

And, perhaps just as bad, whether or not you can reverse your invisibility, once you've committed murder, as Gyges has, even if no one else knows, *you* know, and even if your guilt is never discovered, or punished, your idea of yourself, of who you really are, is completely and permanently changed for the worse.

Much more interesting is the second question: what, even though you knew you couldn't be caught or punished, would you not do? Where would you stop? Would you stop at theft? Would you stop at murder? Why? Why not?

It's said that society has a deal with criminals, which is this: don't get caught. A lot of people don't commit crimes because they know they might be caught, and put in prison for a long time. 'If you can't do the time, don't do the crime', criminals often say to each other. But this is not an ethical argument against doing bad things; it's a rational argument that suggests weighing up the risk-to-reward ratio of doing bad things. Over the past few decades, the number of murders in Western countries has decreased, but this is partly because ambulances have got better at responding to serious assaults. Paramedics now often save people who would in the past have died from their injuries. That doesn't make the people who attacked them ethically better, even though legally they're now thugs rather than murderers. It just means the ambulance service intervened to stop their victims from dying.

This question is interesting because it makes our personal ethics visible. Personal ethics – as distinct from general ethics – are the set of beliefs we hold about ourselves, about what kind of person we are, about how we'd act in certain situations regardless of any written or unwritten laws compelling us to do or not do certain things. It's another way of saying 'your conscience', I suppose. That twinge you occasionally experience when you feel like you might be acting wrongly, whether or not there's any kind of law against what you're doing.

But personal ethics are more correctly defined as your *response* to that twinge of conscience, to the rules you put in place for yourself, whether or not there's anyone watching. Because, of course, there's always someone watching.

You.

6

HOW TO UNDERSTAND A POEM

Part one

Ever heard this? Try reading it aloud:

Divorced Beheaded Died
Divorced Beheaded Survived

DBDDBS. It's an iconic reminder of a teaching style now regarded as old-fashioned. But I bet any adults reading remember it even decades after leaving school. Because it's memorable. To those of you studying the Tudors, I offer the addendum: CAJACC.

It's the initials of Henry VIII's six queens' first names in chronological order, which helps when matching these women's names to their fates.

CAJACC DBDDBS. The Catherines' surnames (Aragon,

Howard and Parr) come in alphabetical order, as do the Annes' (Boleyn and Cleves). So:

Catherine of	Aragon	Divorced
Anne	Boleyn	Beheaded
Jane	Seymour	Died
Anne of	Cleves	Divorced
Catherine	Howard	Beheaded
Catherine	Parr	Survived

I doubt any of my pupils remember CAJACC for more than a few days after their exam. Whereas DBDDBS will probably remain in long-term storage somewhere in your head until the day you die. Why?

It's *memorable*, that's why. Those six words, comprising 13 syllables, arranged in that particular order, contain audible patterns that make them stick in your head. Those patterns are alliteration, rhyme and rhythm, and they are the building blocks of poetry because poetry, unlike the novel, existed long before anyone could actually write anything down. It had to be memorable because that was the only way it could survive. *Poetry is written in ways to make us remember the things we ought not to forget.*

The Iliad, which tells of the siege of Troy, was composed in 1200BC but only written down around 800BC, 400 years later. My copy, translated by Peter Green, is 500 pages long.

That's a lot of memorising. Generations of Greek bards across four centuries carried it safely in their heads, reciting it from memory and making their own additions, before the poet Homer wrote it down. At its most basic functional level, the machinery of poetry is there to make you remember it your whole life.

> Divorced Beheaded Died
> Divorced Beheaded Survived

uses all three of these tricks. There's weighty, serious alliteration in all the Ds and Bs – it sounds like a judge pronouncing a death sentence, which for two of these women it actually was. There's a half rhyme between 'Died' and 'Survived' which catches us by surprise: usually words either rhyme or don't; a half rhyme exists awkwardly midway between these two categories. And there's a regular rhythm of alternating BEATS (the SYLLables that our VOICes NATurally STRESS when we READ them aLOUD, which I've ALso CAPitalised beLOW), a rhythm which is interrupted at the end of the second line. Try saying it out loud, it goes:

te-TUM	te-TUM	te-TUM
di-VORCED	be-HEAD-	-ed DIED
te-TUM	te-TUM	te-te-TUM
di-VORCED	be-HEAD-	-ed sur-VIVED

– all until that extra syllable in the last word, 'Survived', where we were expecting another 'Died' to complete the second line's repetition of the first line. All of this underlines that half rhyme, and reminds us how lucky Henry's last wife was to outlive her tyrant of a husband.

Alliteration

Alliteration was really popular a thousand years ago in Old English (i.e. pre-1066) poems like *Beowulf*, which is about an almost superhuman hero's fight with a terrifying cannibal called Grendel, whom we first see making his brutal nightly raid on a neighbouring king's feasting hall:

> Greedy and grim, he grabbed 30 men
> From their resting places and rushed to his lair,
> Flushed up and inflamed from the raid,
> Blundering back with the butchered corpses.[1]

Listen to how Grendel's ghastly crimes are underlined by the way the consonants catch in your throat when you read the lines aloud: 'Gr… gr… gr…/ r… r… …sh…/ F… …sh… f…/ B… b… b…'

Similarly, lots of 'ss' (aka sibillance) suggests something serpentine and sinister, like Satan in John Milton's *Paradise*

[1] From Seamus Heaney's fantastic translation of *Beowulf.*

Lost, who disguises himself as a snake to tempt Eve with the apple: 'serpent, subtlest beast of all the field'. Listen to the seductive syllables of Rudyard Kipling's rock python Kaa in Walt Disney's film of *The Jungle Book*. Sssss.

And whether it's describing villains or heroes, there's something about alliteration that just sounds *right*. Peter Parker and Clark Kent and Bruce Banner all have a ring about them. You just know there's something special about those guys.

Rhyme

Speaking of Milton, here's a WH Auden poem:

John Milton
Never stayed at a Hilton
Hotel
Which was just as well.

The rhyme scheme is simple and jokey. It's satisfying to our ears when we hear the payoff – which was set up by the first line's rhyme ('Milton') – at the end of the second line ('Hilton'). Though the lines are (surprisingly) of different lengths, the first and second lines rhyme, and so do the third and fourth ones. To keep track, we allocate a letter of the alphabet to pairs of lines that rhyme: this four-line poem's rhyme scheme is AABB:

John Milton	A
Never stayed at a Hilton	A
Hotel	B
Which was just as well.	B

The first rhyme, 'Milton'/ 'Hilton', humorously pairs up two total opposites. John Milton was a blind, Puritan 17th-century poet who wrote *Paradise Lost* 'to explain the ways of God to Man'. Hilton is a modern international hotel chain with cable TV and minibars in every room. So these two words, which Auden links together in our heads by their similar sounds, don't go together at all – and it's by linking them in this way that the *contrast* between the two is brought out more strongly. We're inclined to agree with the poet – Milton probably wouldn't have liked a Hilton.

Here's the opening stanza of a longer poem, also by Auden, about a long and difficult sea journey to find the ancient lost city of Atlantis. Read it first, as always, for the sense of what the poet is actually trying to say. But keep half an ear out for the rhyme scheme.

Is it straightforward and jokey, like 'Milton'/ 'Hilton', 'Hotel'/ 'well'?

Or is it more complicated than that?

Atlantis

Being set on the idea
Of getting to Atlantis,
You have discovered of course
Only the Ship of Fools is
Making the voyage this year,
As gales of abnormal force
Are predicted, and that you
Must therefore be ready to
Behave absurdly enough
To pass for one of The Boys,
At least appearing to love
Hard liquor, horseplay and noise.

The rhyme scheme is ABCBACDDEFEF. Why so complex? Well, sea journeys in the ancient world were dangerous and uncertain. You were relying entirely on the wind and could easily get blown completely off course. On the next page is the route taken after the fall of Troy by the Greek hero Odysseus to Ithaca, to get home. Take a look.

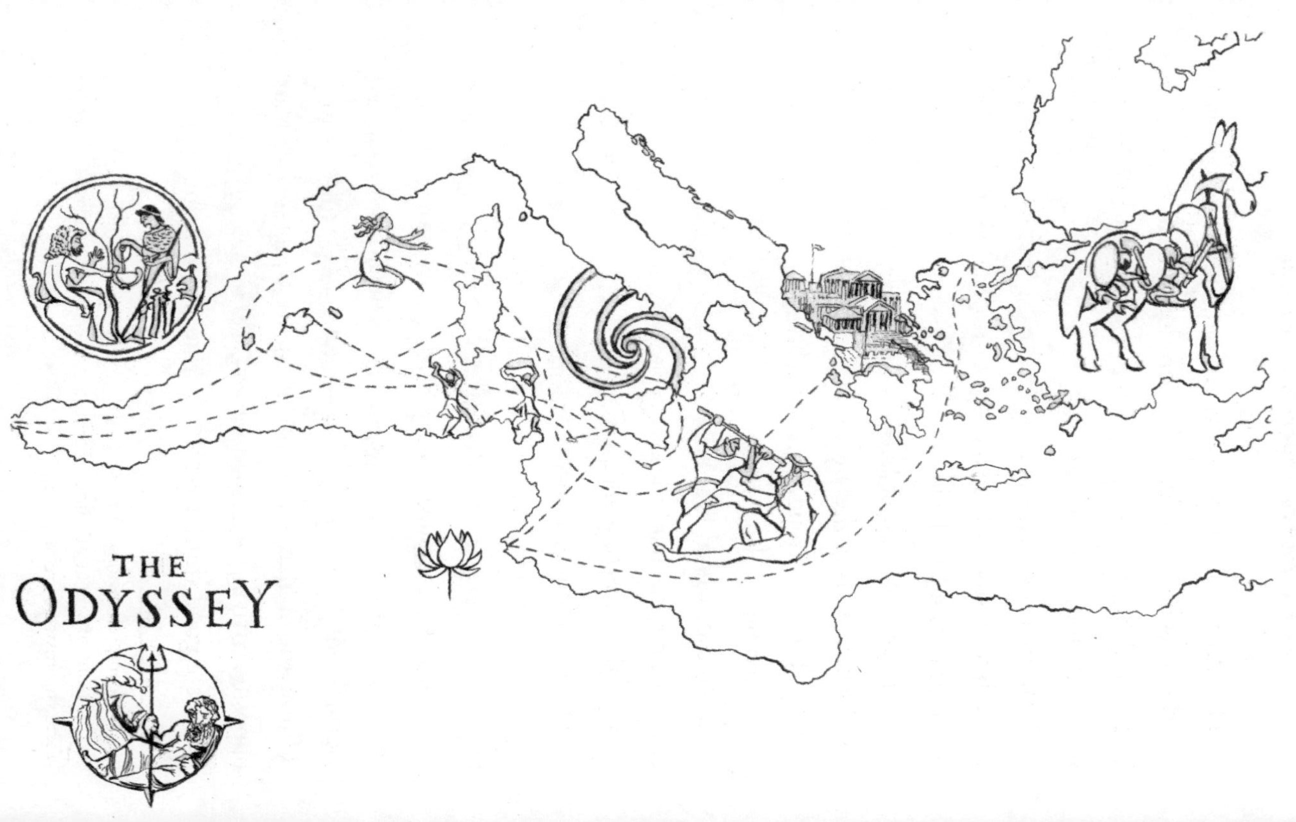
THE
ODYSSEY

He rather took the long way around, didn't he? Likewise, the rhyme scheme in Auden's poem loops back on itself in bigger and bigger circles, like the ripples a pebble makes when it's dropped into water.

Read that opening stanza aloud again, and listen out for the different kinds of rhymes that Auden uses to link the words at the end of the lines.[2]

There are a couple of half rhymes ('Atlantis/is'; 'enough/love') which adds to the uncertainty – we were expecting full rhymes. There's a strong rhyme at the end – 'Boys' is not only capitalised but is also rhymed with 'noise', implying there is some kind of causal link between the two – that the presence of *boys* inevitably leads to the production of *noise* – a suggestion which, while perhaps slightly sexist, isn't in my experience an outrageously unfair one.

Like alliteration, rhyming *matches* words: they either go together or – especially with half rhymes – are opposites. It's a way of making you subconsciously compare them. A recent government categorised people as 'strivers' or 'skivers', with no room in the middle. As with 'Milton'/'Hilton', the similar sounds actually create in our heads a binary opposite. 'Striving' – trying hard to become rich and successful – is a good thing that we approve of, so it must follow

[2] In any comprehension exam, poetry or prose, you should always keep the text in front of you at all times. Rip the staples out if you have to. That's where the answers are, after all.

that anyone who isn't striving, who is poor or doesn't have a job, must be 'skiving', which is a bad thing, that we despise.

In 'Wonderful World' Sam Cooke sings:

Don't know much about alge*bra*
Don't know what a slide rule is *for*

This song is sung by an uneducated young black man in the southern United States in 1962 to woo a potential girlfriend. I don't care about all this book-learning stuff, he's saying – there's more to life than that. And by rhyming 'algebra' with 'for' he is deliberately showing off his uneducated accent. They don't rhyme when we say them out loud, but when Cooke sings it in his strong southern accent, that 'for' comes out as 'fuh'– a perfect rhyme with the 'uh' sound at the end of 'algebra'. So this rhyme doesn't just show off his verbal wit to compensate for his lack of education, it also makes a defiant virtue of the outsider status that his accent gives him.

Marvin Gaye pulls a similar trick in this opening to one of his greatest songs:

Baby, I'm hot just like an *oven*
I need some *loving*

Sometimes, though, rhyme is just there for the sheer pleasure of the sound. Mariah Carey in 'We Belong Together', another pop song, manages to be witty and heartbroken at the same time:

I'm feeling all out of my *element*
Throwing things, crying, trying to figure out where the *hell I went*
Wrong.

Rhythm

The Latin word *carmen* means both 'song' and 'poem', which is my excuse for dropping in those song lyrics above. It also reminds us that songs and poems have one thing in common – and that without it, they would not be songs and poems. That thing is rhythm. Poems don't *have* to rhyme, and they don't need alliteration, to be poems. But rhythm *is* essential, even if a clear meter (rhythmical pattern) can be hard to find in some modern poems. Lineation is essential too – all poems are written in lines – on which more later.

Below is the most famous line in English poetry. The te-TUMs are marked out using the standard notation for unstressed and stressed syllables. I've also capitalised the stressed syllables so you really hear them. Try reading it aloud and really hearing which syllables your voice naturally lands on more heavily.

x /	x /	x /	/ x	x / x
To BE,	or NOT	to BE,	THAT is	the QUEStion

Key:

x = unstressed syllable (also known as te)

/ = stressed syllable (aka a BEAT, aka TUM)

x / = iamb (te-TUM)

/ **x** = trochee (TUM-te)

The pattern of this line is iambic pentameter,[3] which means five iambs on one line, and which is the most popular rhythm in English poetry, because it is generally thought:

x /	x /	x /	x /	x /
to be	the clos-	-est thing	to nor-	-mal speech

The line immediately above is also iambic pentameter, five iambs in a row, which you'll hear if you read it aloud. Te-TUM Te-TUM Te-TUM Te-TUM Te-TUM. When reading poetry, try drawing in the xs and /s for yourself. Read interesting or difficult bits aloud. Underline them, scribble a word or two.[4]

---

3 Actually, it's not exactly standard iambic pentameter because of the addition of that final unstressed syllable, giving it what is sometimes called (sorry) a 'weak' or 'feminine' ending.

4 Studies show that writing by hand embeds words in the memory.

Interpreting rhythm

And this is as far as most students take it, which is a shame, because no examiner will ask you simply whether a poem was written in iambic pentameter or not. Appreciating a poem's rhythm isn't just about marking down regular patterns with xs and /s. It's about the irregular bits – and how those bits affect the meaning of the poem. You've got to look for where the structure changes and the whole damn thing breaks down. You've got to find the places where the messy emotions of the real world break through the poem's strict formality. That's the bit to mine for marks, that's where the gold is buried.

x /	x /	x /	/ x	x / x
To be,	or not	to be,	that is	the question

'To be, or not to be'. These are the words of Hamlet, a suicidal man whose regular thoughts are being brutally interrupted by one irregular thought: of taking his own life. 'THAT is the question', he shouts, spoiling the three regular iambs with a trochee (/ x), which is the exact opposite of the expected iamb (x /). The rhythm is jarring and disturbing, like a jabbed finger – but it's also appropriate in terms of what's going on in the play, which is that a man is obsessing over killing himself. Dark, disturbing stuff.

As Jonas Salk, the creator of the polio vaccine, observed, it's when something stops working that you see how it works the rest of the time. With rhyme and rhythm you must work out the underlying pattern, then focus on the places where that pattern breaks down: these are the parts where the poem's meaning reveals itself.

Here's Auden again, writing about a train. Try marking the /s (there are four stressed syllables on each line) and the xs (there are six unstressed syllables on each line) before you look at the answers below to check your work. Maybe use pencil, so you can erase it for the next person (especially if this is a library book).

This is the	Night Mail	crossing the	Border,
Bringing the	cheque and the	Postal	Order

/ x x	/ x	/ x x	/ x
This is the	Night Mail	crossing the	Border,
/ x x	/ x x	/ x	/ x
Bringing the	cheque and the	Postal	Order

Hold out your left index finger. A dactyl, the Ancient Greek word for finger, has the same pattern as the three bones in your left index finger: big-small-small, or

/ x x

So these two lines are a mixture of dactyls

/ x x

and trochees

/ x

but they're arranged differently on each of the two lines:

dactyl	trochee	dactyl	trochee
This is the	Night Mail	crossing the	Border,
dactyl	dactyl	trochee	trochee
Bringing the	cheque and the	Postal	Order

And if you read Auden's lines aloud again:

This is the Night Mail crossing the Border,
Bringing the cheque and the Postal Order

You can hear that regular-irregular rhythm as mimicking the movement of a train shuttling along on its tracks. Again, the poem's meter (another word for rhythm) imitates the feeling of what the words themselves describe – they are imitative, or mimetic, of the poem's subject.

So it's not all about the iamb (x /). The inverted iamb, or trochee (/ x) that we met in the middle of that Shakespeare line ('THAT IS the question') can, if used repeatedly provide an even stronger driving forward movement than the iamb (x /). Whether made of iambs, trochees, dactyls or free verse, a poem's rhythm drives it; it's its irregular bits that slow and complicate.

Here's William Blake. Please read him aloud.

/ x	/ x	/ x	/
Tyger,	tyger	burning	bright,
/ x	/ x	/ x	/
In the	forests	of the	night

Note how the rhythmic power of the first line forces us to read the second line in exactly the same trochaic alternating pattern, whereas, if we had come across that phrase in a novel or a newspaper we would more naturally read it like this, with only two stressed syllables instead of four: again, read this aloud like you're in conversation with someone:

x x	/ x	x x	/
In the	forests	of the	night

But the iamb is endlessly adaptable and manages a similar driving effect in Chuck Berry's 'Johnny B. Goode'. (Google it.) Actually, you'll notice that its first line is made up of iambs (x /), and the second line is trochees (/ x). But they're both built on six stressed syllables alternating with unstressed ones.

Again, read these lines aloud to get the full effect. Fill in the last four lines yourself, if you want.

/ /	x / x / x	/ x	/ x /
Deep down	in Lou'siana	close to	New Orleans
/ x	x / x	/ x /	x / x /
Way back	up in the	woods among	the evergreens
There stood	a log cabin	made of	earth and wood
Where lived	a country	boy named	Johnny B. Goode
Who never	ever learned	to read and	write so well
But he	could play a	guitar just like	ringin' a bell.

Alliteration, rhyme and rhythm all together at once

Here's a line from 'The Windhover' by the Victorian poet Gerard Manley Hopkins, about the thrill of watching a kestrel (a kind of falcon) hovering in the air motionless as it hunts. Again, read it out loud.

x /	x /	x /	x x /
My heart	in hid-	-ing stirred	for a bird

Hopkins uses alliteration, rhyme (although it's internal to the line) and a regular rhythm that suddenly with a stutter, or perhaps a flutter, changes at the end. Try reading that sentence while omitting the word 'for' – and it is four perfect iambs.

x /	x /	x /	x /
My heart	in hid-	-ing stirred	a bird

Five iambs in one line, as we've seen, are called iambic pentameter; four are tetrameter; three trimeter. But the regularity of a metrical scheme is not the point; the point is the flaw in that scheme, the one that draws your ear to it. That extra beat (the unstressed syllable 'for') delays by one suspenseful moment the revealing of the poet's longed-for object – the 'bird' – as well as surprising us with a rhyme that's not (as usual) between two lines, but within one (this is called an internal rhyme).

Both the heartfelt longing and sharp surprise seem to come from the poet's wonder at the raptor's ruthless beauty – instead of being functions of rhythm and rhyme. In fact, these tricks of form are there to subtly underline the content of the poem – the thoughts and feelings of the poet.

As I've mentioned earlier (p 136), *ars est celare artem*: 'art' means concealing art. If we can see how a magician does his tricks we are less amazed by them. Likewise, the poet must both use his art and hide it from us if we are to be truly moved by his words. The truest poetry is the most feigning. It's our job as critics to uncover the tricks the poet has buried under a surface of words.

Lineation and stanzas

The other thing that makes a poem a poem is lineation. Poetry is written in lines, but English *means* in sentences – sentences that sometimes run-on over several lines and stop suddenly partway through. Poets have always exploited this difference to change their sentences' meanings by breaking them up across lines, to conjure up cliffhangers or suddenly switch the point of attack. You know you're reading a poem rather than a novel or a newspaper when it comes in lines that
end before the page runs
out. This technique, of dropping
down a line in the middle of a sentence in ways that can surprise you with the next word, is called enjambment. It's sometimes associated with the feeling that you're
falling.

Endstopping is the opposite of enjambment, where every line ends with a pause and usually a piece of punctuation.

It can be a bit bland and repetitive as in William McGonagall's notorious 'The Tay Bridge Disaster', which strains for tragedy (pathos) but ends up as unintentional comedy (bathos):

As soon as the catastrophe came to be known,
The alarm from mouth to mouth was blown,
And the cry rang out all o'er the town,
Good Heavens! the Tay Bridge is blown down!

Endstopped lines are clearer, and carry a certain authority and clarity. Shakespeare's kings often speak this way, unless they're upset or angry (which is often).

Stanza is the Italian word for 'room', and it means the same as 'verse'. A stanza is usually a set number of lines long, with the same rhythm and rhyme scheme as the other stanzas that make up the poem. Like verses in songs, paragraphs in prose, and scenes in films and plays, stanzas are units of meaning that can be understood separately but go together to make up a larger whole. A poem's sentences can be enjambed across stanzas as well as over lines, so they're not always entirely self-contained units. Many poems don't have stanzas at all.

Metaphors and similes

Apart from lineation and stanzas, which affect the poem's visual shape on the page, all of the formal effects we've looked at so far have to do with the way poems *sound*. Imagery, meaning metaphors and similes, is different – it's seen: imaginary, but visible in the mind's eye of the reader. You can think of imagery as the mental pictures made by sparks flying when two different meanings rub up against, or even crash into each other.

- The moon *is like* a balloon. *Simile*. It's the Latin word for 'similar thing'.
- The moon *is* a balloon. *Metaphor*. From the Greek word *meta-pherein*, meaning 'to carry away'. A metaphor literally carries off the meaning from one word and applies it to another. I once saw a truck in Athens that had 'METAPHORS' written on the side. It was a removal lorry.

Metaphors are stronger than similes, because they break the truth, whereas similes only bend it. If similes are like borrowing, metaphor is theft. But, as the narrator in Mark Haddon's *The Curious Incident of the Dog in the Night-Time* says, he prefers similes. This is because similes are true (the moon *<u>is</u> like* a balloon – it's round and in the sky), and metaphors are lies (the moon *<u>is not</u>*, in fact, a balloon).

The American poet Randall Jarrell fought in the Second World War and didn't particularly enjoy it. In 'Losses', he writes:

In bombers named for girls, we burned
The cities we had learned about in school

In another of his poems, 'The Lullaby', Randall bemoans a soldier's lot in a powerful double *simile*:

lied to *like a child*, cursed *like a beast.*

But it's the closing *simile-metaphor*, one-two punch that really hits home:

And his dull torment mottles *like a fly's*
The lying *amber of the histories.*

The simile 'like a fly's' is not comparing a soldier to a fly – note the two possessives, 'his' and 'fly's', at either end of the first line. Instead it's comparing a soldier's suffering to a fly's suffering, thereby making us consider one of the few things these two creatures have in common: each feels pain. Both of their torments are described as 'dull', a word that can mean 'mild' (which doesn't seem to fit, given the horrors of human warfare and of life in the insect world); or 'boring' (whether for the one suffering the torment or for us witnessing it); or 'muffled and indistinct'.

This last definition seems the best fit. As the American comedian Mitch Hedberg said, 'If fish could scream, the ocean would be loud as shit'. Well, flies can't scream – and neither, Jarrell suggests here, can soldiers. While that's not literally true (hence the simile '*like* a fly's'), it seems fair to say that the agonies of the average soldier, one of millions in the field, went largely unheard. The Americans who fought in World War Two had come through the Great Depression of the 1930s: many were illiterate. These soldiers' agonies, Jarrell is saying, went as unexpressed and unheard as a fly's.

To 'mottle' means to stain something of one pure colour with spots or streaks of another – so this fly is literally 'the fly in the ointment'. The poet compares these two mottlings (the soldier's 'torment' and fly's) with a simile; then in the second line he uses the power of metaphor to contrast the pure things which are spoiled by them. Amber and history are the prized by-products of two natural processes. A tree's resin drips down its bark, sometimes engulfing unwitting flies, and over millions of years fossilises into a solid but translucent block. The flies are thus imprisoned for all time in a trinket, the amber block made more valuable by their presence, to be passed around and admired by enthusiasts.[5]

Likewise, we would rather admire the big narratives of human history – formed over millennia by our apparently incurable appetite for killing each other – than hear the small

[5] Watch the first two minutes of Steven Spielberg's *Jurassic Park* for possible future uses of prehistoric flies preserved in amber.

torments of those who have been blamelessly caught up in them.

Finally, and most cruelly, this version of history is 'lying' anyway – unlike the translucent amber which clearly displays the fly's death. Jarrell's use of the plural 'histories' suggests the somewhat fictionalised *Histories* of Herodotus and Shakespeare and Tacitus, and reminds us that its Latin origin word *historiae* can refer both to factual 'histories' and to fabricated 'stories'. The soldier, then, is denied even the 'truthful' commemoration in fossilised amber which is granted the fly. Think of that next time you pass a war memorial.

Word choice

In 1066 a French-speaking aristocracy conquered this largely Germanic (Old English)-speaking island and ordered their dinner in French: *boeuf*, *porc* and *mouton*. But the Germanic-speaking peasants serving them only knew Germanic (Old English) words like cow, pig and sheep. So the new French words (beef, pork and mutton) became the names of the meats served to a Norman lord, and the Germanic words (cow, pig and sheep) became the names of the live animals to be slaughtered by the Anglo-Saxon peasants for the new masters' tables.

And so a class divide grew up between the posh Romance (i.e. French or Latin) words and the crude Germanic words that together make up the English language as we use it today. Even though they mean almost the same thing, 'beautiful' (French) is somehow better than 'pretty' (Germanic). Romance words ('revolution', 'liberty', 'essence') tend to be polysyllabic (i.e. long) and *'of the mind'*, whereas Germanic words ('fight', 'hurt', 'crunch') are short and *'of the body'*. Every swear word (or, in Old English, *schitworde*) worth knowing is originally Germanic (you can supply your own list). Whereas, most ideas or inventions worth knowing about – capitalism, democracy, antibiotics – have Romance or Greek names.

Of course, there are many words in English for the same thing. 'Corporeal' (Romance) means the same as 'bodily' (Germanic), it's just that the first one sounds posher and cleverer, but also flimsier and less sincere. So 'I love you' (Germanic) is better and more commonly said than 'I adore you' (French), because it seems to come from the heart rather than the head. On the other hand, 'economic analysis' (Romance) sounds more convincing than 'gold thinking' (Germanic) – when it comes to money, head beats heart. If you can recognise, or guess – by its sound or length or tone – the *origin* (which is a Romance word) of a *word* (a Germanic word), you can also make inferences about whether the poet wants you to think elegant, aristocratic thoughts (head), or instead feel basic bodily things (heart).

Similarly, look out for negative or pejorative language (from the Latin *peior*, meaning 'worse'); and also its opposite – positive or meliorative language. This applies particularly to adjectives, which beneath their surface meaning can convey the poet's like or dislike of the thing being described:

Svelte, slim, slender	Positive
Thin	Neutral
Skinny, bony, emaciated	Pejorative

All the above words mean the same thing, but each expresses a different attitude to that thing. The writer's word choice shows how he really feels about what he is describing: it is closely related to tone, on which more later.

Be patient and be on the lookout for language being used to provoke a specific emotional response. If at a funeral we say someone 'passed away' rather than 'died', we're using a euphemism (Greek for 'speaking well') to soften our words out of respect for the bereaved family. We made that *word choice* (one could even call 'passed away' a metaphor) to strike the appropriate *tone*, in order to create with our words a consoling *mood* to soothe people in pain. Likewise, the poet picks his or her words carefully to create images, associations and emotions in your head that change how you understand the poem.

So. You're nearly at the end of part one. Phew, well done, etc. Let's conclude with some thoughts on a couple of murderers.

Narrator and character

When you read a poem, always ask yourself – *Who is talking?* Who is the narrator? What can you tell about him based on what he says and how he says it? Is the narrator also the main character of the poem? If so, what is his attitude to himself, based on how he describes himself? If narrator and character are two different people, how does one narrate the other? What is their relationship? What do they think of each other? How do they differ?

In Robert Browning's 'My Last Duchess', an Italian Renaissance duke who may or may not have murdered his dead wife seems to boast of his crime to the matchmaker who is fixing him up with his next wife. (Bear in mind too that the poet is a different person again from either the narrator or the character. Luckily for his poet wife Elizabeth Barrett-Browning, Robert Browning the poet was not a wife-killer.)

The duke, though, who is the poem's narrator and its main character, may be a murderer and more, as we realise when he describes how angry it made him when his dead duchess smiled at other men:

> Oh sir, she smiled, no doubt
> Whene'er I passed her; but who passed without
> Much the same smile? This grew; I gave commands;
> Then all smiles stopped together.

To be a murderer is one thing; to murder a loved one is quite another; but to boast of murdering them, and to boast of it to the marriage broker you have hired to find your next wife, suggests a person either incapable of recognising evil, or one who delights in it. The character the duke reveals as the poem's narrator is that of a psychopath, someone who believes that other human beings exist only for his convenience. And his arrogance in boasting of his true nature to the marriage broker, unafraid of any consequences, shows us that he is a man who believes he cannot be stopped.

Mood and tone

Finally, consider the poem's mood – what is its atmosphere, in both the inner headspace of the narrator, and the outer space of the real world as it exists in the poem? Which emotions does it make you feel? And what is the speaker's tone, his attitude to the poem's subject? Think about the actual tone of voice it should be read in – you'll understand better what the poet's really trying to say.

Siegfried Sassoon's poem 'The General' compares the reputation among his men of a well-liked but incompetent First World War commander with the actual effect that his wrong-headed strategy has on them:

> "He's a cheery old card," grunted Harry to Jack
> As they slogged up to Arras with rifle and pack.
> But he did for them both by his plan of attack.

The mood is initially, like the general of the title, 'cheery'. The rhyme helps too – the AA rhymed couplet of 'Jack' and 'pack' – which is simple and upbeat. Despite the 'slog' of war, 'Harry' and 'Jack' (such jolly names!) really like their boss.

Then, abruptly, the mood sours with the third line, and the poet's (rather than the two soldiers') true attitude to this idiot is revealed by his brutally harsh tone: 'he did for them both'. 'Jack' and 'pack' get a third rhyme, unusually, which comes as a horrible surprise for the two men: 'attack'. Like a smile pasted unconvincingly over a frown, the jaunty rhyme scheme of 'Jack'/ 'pack'/ 'attack' actually *emphasises* the grim tone of the last line by contrasting so strongly with it.

Similarly, consider this children's nursery rhyme:

Ring a ring of roses,
A pocket full of posies,
A-tishoo! A-tishoo!
We all fall down.

It all sounds jolly enough, but probably has its origin in pagan myth, or in religious oppression that forbade all dancing, or in the outbreaks of bubonic plague that killed 200 million people worldwide between the 14th and 18th centuries. Not so jolly after all.

Likewise, Sassoon's changing tone in 'The General' shows that he regards the 'cheery' commander, who threw Harry and Jack's lives away without a thought, as being criminally negligent, and therefore little better than a murderer.

Prose: a brief intermission

If you can play snooker you can play pool. The reverse is not necessarily true: snooker is a similar but much harder game.

If you can analyse poetry, you can analyse prose. The reverse is not necessarily true: poetry is a similar, but much harder game.

It is language turned up to the highest difficulty setting. Almost everything said here about poetry criticism also applies to prose criticism. But poetry is harder, which is why I'm focusing on it. Plus, as we all know, books about poetry always sell by the truckload.

Alliteration (remember Peter Parker and Clark Kent?) exists in prose too, and so does rhyme, at times. Prose also has its own rhythm, as in the closing sentence of F Scott Fitzgerald's novel *The Great Gatsby*:

/ x	/ x	/ x	/ x	/ x
So we	beat on,	boats a-	-gainst the	current,
/	/	/	x x /	x x /
borne	back	cease-	-lessly in-	-to the past.

The optimistic regular trochees of first 'line' here are like the oarstrokes of a rower who is confident, despite the current being against his boat. The second line is where he comes unstuck – three desperate oarstrokes in quick succession, and then two more strokes, but further apart than before, slower and weaker, his strength exhausted.

Prose likewise demands we consider its metaphors and similes, word choice, narrators and characters, mood and tone.[6] Prose *is* different from poetry, of course: plainer, more straightforward, less dense (which is why in an exam you'll spend the same time on a 14-line poem as on a 100-line extract from a novel). Because of this, some kinds of writing[7] work better in prose: satire, for example, which started in Ancient Rome as a subset of poetry but had migrated to prose by 1729 when Jonathan Swift's prose pamphlet 'A Modest Proposal' caused an uproar. Swift's proposal was that starving Irish families made poor by British economic policies could earn much-needed money by selling their babies to rich Englishmen who would then eat them. It's a joke, of course. But a joke with a point. Look at the narrator – who is talking? Swift was an Irishman. Ireland was then a British colony. Why would an Irishman make such a tasteless joke about his own countrymen? His tone is straightfaced and 'modest', despite

---

[6] Lineation and stanzas are out, you'll be pleased to hear.

[7] Use the Romance word *genres* instead of 'kinds of writing' if you want to sound clever.

the exaggerated, absurd content. What is behind it? Well, this reasonable tone is satirising – attacking, really – not his own people, but the 'reasonable' attitudes of the British ruling class whose policies were causing his country's impoverishment. The mood behind Swift's joke is one of deep anger. *Stop hurting my people*, is what he is really saying.

Poetry: part two

The English poet Philip Larkin once said that there are only two things you can do with a poem: 'Read it to yourself, or read it out loud.' Unlike novels,[8] poetry existed before writing. Supposedly the first man who could read to himself without moving his lips was Bishop Ambrose of Milan in the fourth century CE. So for all but the past 1600 years of poetry's many millennia, poetry was read aloud even when enough books existed that it no longer had to be declaimed from memory.

Read it out loud

So read it aloud. You can't do this in an exam, but every other time you read a poem, you can. You wouldn't sit there and just

[8] A 300-year-old form – have a look at *Robinson Crusoe* for an example of an early novel, or skip forward 100 years to *Treasure Island* if you get bored.

read sheet music: if you want to experience music, you have to play it. Likewise, working out how to read aloud Larkin's deceptively simple lines so that they sound right is also the work of understanding his complex syntax. What's this bit really saying? Having to perform a poem forces you to think about the emotion you need to project with your voice onto each and every line. This is how actors prepare.

And you must learn by heart at least one poem. How poetry works and what it is for, its form and its content, are at heart the same thing – to make you remember. Without showing off too much, I can say that every line of poetry in part one of this chapter was quoted from memory. I never sat down to learn any of them. I remembered these words simply because something about them stayed with me at the time, and they have been rattling around in my brain ever since. Poetry is written in ways to make us remember the things we ought not to forget.

According to Albert Einstein, education is what you still remember when you have forgotten what you learned in school. And poetry is ultimately *about* the human capacity to remember. In the long hard millennia before writing was invented, poetry only existed within human memory. Memorise a poem and it's yours forever.

Read it to yourself

I suggest you read alone in a room with the door closed. No screens should be present. Your phone, if you have one, should be turned off and in another room. You'll need ten undistracted minutes of total focus to really get under the skin of the poem. What's it about? Read it first for its content, before you start to worry about form (i.e. everything discussed in part one). That way, you're already considering *what* it's about while you're examining *how* it works on a technical level.

Your first experience of a poem should ignore all the technical stuff. Instead use empathy, or as my mother taught it to me, The I Test: Ask yourself, 'How would I feel if I were in this situation?'. Put yourself in the shoes of the person who is speaking to you directly through these lines.

Then you can read it for meter (five-beat pentameter? Four-beat tetrameter? Something else?), and mark where the rhythm breaks down. Underline interesting or difficult phrases or words (they are often one and the same thing). Re-read those parts especially. What about imagery? The other senses? Read the whole thing again. Who is talking? How are they talking? How does all this affect the meaning of each line, each word? Where do form and content fit? Where do they clash?

We'll get to all that. Welcome to part two.

Content

So you've now got a better chance of recognising all the poetic techniques outlined in part one, but what do they actually do? What do they actually mean? When you take a car apart, you need to know more than which bit is the carburettor and where the power steering is. You need to know how each part actually works, and how, together, they make the car go. Form is the umbrella term for all the techniques discussed in part one, and more besides. It is every word choice that a poet makes. It is the box they pour their heart into.

A poem is a machine for meaning, with many moving parts, but it still needs something driving it. The heart of the poem – what the poet is thinking, how he or she feels, what the poem is *about* – is the content. Form and content are the two basic categories that together comprise any work of art. They are opposites – form is the *how*, and content is the *what* – but they are always intertwined.

That's because how you say something always influences what you say, or at least how it is received. 'The message *is* the medium', as Marshall McLuhan said. Sarcasm is a function of form, for example: if you say 'That's a *really* nice hat', how you said '*really*' might show you actually meant the opposite of what you said. Likewise with understatement: 'Not *bad*,' you might say, when someone scores a brilliant goal against your team. Content is what you should focus on when you first look at a poem, because that's what it's actually about, and because in an exam it's where most of the marks are.

Content is hard to generalise about, though, to make rules for, as we did with form. Because the content of poetry is *life*. Poetry, like all literature, is *equipment for living* – it is, quite simply, experience and advice from someone who has been there before, wherever *there* might be. Now, you might reasonably argue that JRR Tolkien never visited Middle Earth, and that any guidance that came from there would be specific to hobbits. But Tolkien did live at a time when the peace and prosperity of the West were threatened by a Dark Lord in the East,[9] his spies[10] everywhere, his every bidding done by the undead vassal kings[11] of the surrounding lands. And the advice an observant reader will take from *The Lord of the Rings* – to gather allies, to be resourceful, to be aware of one's limitations, to be courageous in the face of trouble – is good advice for anyone living through dark times, fictitious or not.

Life, as you've probably noticed, is messy, complex and unpredictable. If you're reading this aged 13, however packed those years have been, you won't have experienced all that much of it. You don't need to. You just need to be willing to

---

[9] Joseph Stalin.

[10] The NKVD, later the KGB, currently the FSB (Federal Security Bureau). Star alumnus Vladimir Putin. Of course the British (MI6) and Americans (CIA) also did their share of spying during the Cold War. Read John Le Carré's great novel *Tinker, Tailor, Soldier, Spy* – or Google 'The Cambridge Ring' if you want facts.

[11] The leaders of the other Warsaw Pact countries.

imagine someone else's experience of it. A lot of poets wrote their greatest stuff young; many of them died young too, like John Keats (at 25) and Percy Shelley (at 29). Here's their fellow Romantic poet William Wordsworth with his definition of poetry:

> Poetry is the spontaneous overflow of powerful feelings: it takes its origin from emotion recollected in tranquillity.

Literature shows us the other possible lives, for good or ill, that we might lead, and helps us choose the good. Reading literature means using imagination and empathy to put yourself into that person's life. Treat a poem like meeting another person for the first time. There's probably more to them than meets the eye.

The two questions

There are only two questions you need to answer about any poem:

- What's it about?
  Content
- What's it *really* about?
  Form and content together

The first question will be apparent after one or two readings. This is the content of the poem, what it's about on the surface, what the story is.

Answering the second question might take five or ten readings. This is why I told you all the stuff beforehand about form. Every aspect of a poem's machinery is connected to and influenced by every other aspect: you need to study all its mechanics to see how its parts fit together and work together, to create meaning.

Five questions

This 'two questions' lark is all very well, you might say, but most English scholarship exams ask more than two questions about the poem they've set. You're right – somewhere between five and ten is standard. But if you look at what's behind any exam question, you'll find it's asking about either form or content, or about both at once. You need to dig into the questions asked about it as deeply as you do into the text of the poem set. What are they really asking?

The key thing for all exams, but especially scholarship ones, is to bear in mind who set the paper. English teachers – all of them, but at the top schools especially – are creatures of exquisite taste and considerable reading. The poems set will be rich texts with lots of marks available for the student willing to dig. They will also be difficult. As TS Eliot wrote in 1921:

> ... poets in our civilisation, as it exists at present, must be *difficult*.

The poems will be difficult. The questions will be difficult. Digging will be necessary.

Many schools post past papers on their websites. Use them. The papers set in these schools' scholarship exams are an invaluable resource for anyone sitting any English exam. Students contemplating them should attempt many practice papers. Only later on should these be completed under timed conditions: get it right first; then get fast.

Here, then, are five questions on poems taken from various schools' scholarship exams (two from Eton, two from Oundle, one from Winchester). The words you should focus on are in *italics*. You haven't read the poems so you can't answer these questions on them. You can, though, answer this crucial one: Is the question asking you to comment on the poem's *form*, or on its *content*? Or on its *form* and *content* together? Circle the *(F)*, the *(C)* or the *(F+C)* alongside each question accordingly. Then check your answers at the bottom of the next page.

1. Write down an example of alliteration and explain its effect. [Eton, 2014] *(F)* *(C)* *(F+C)*
2. Summarise the boy's attitude to the 'children who were rough'. [Eton, 2014] *(F)* *(C)* *(F+C)*

3. Why do you think the second stanza is the only one which does not rhyme? [Oundle, 2013]
   (F) (C) (F+C)
4. The lines are very loose in terms of meter, almost prose-like, and there is a great deal of enjambment. Why do you think the poet chose to write in this style? [Oundle, 2013] *(F) (C) (F+C)*
5. Describe in your own words the poet's attitude towards the rat. [Winchester, 2015]
   (F) (C) (F+C)

Did you get five out of five?[12] I'm not 100% sure I did, and I set the test. It's not a science. But you get the idea.

Form and content, though useful categories for explaining how poems create meaning and emotion, are in the end impossible to separate. Reading poetry well means understanding the techniques discussed in part one *and* their effects on its meaning. It also means keeping your antennae up (What's it *really* about?), and giving your considered impression. With, brief, relevant quotations from the text.

These five questions suggest that most of the available marks in these exams are for understanding content. This is true. But for the rest you need to understand form – and how it affects content. Those marks are by far the hardest ones

[12] Answers: 1) F+C, 2) C, 3) F+C, 4) F+C, 5) C

to get. They are the difference between a low-to-middling B, and a clear A. And we didn't get into this for a low-to-middling B. 100% is as possible in an English exam as in any other subject. You just need a method. Here is that method.

The ten reads

'Poetry must almost successfully resist comprehension' as the poet and teacher Mr MacKinnon cheerfully told our A-level class in 1995 (his complex, chatty poetry is occasionally set for scholarship exams). Mr MacKinnon would distribute a photocopied poem, then leave the classroom for the first ten minutes of a 40-minute lesson, returning to open the discussion with the words 'So. What did you make of that?'.

Ten minutes is a long time to be left with a 14-line poem (a sonnet, for example). You have nothing else to do but read it again and again, ten times or more. It can be tough going if the poem doesn't grab you. But it's always instructive.

If you're used to having things explained for you, it's initially disconcerting. The bar for insightful observations is set fairly high. So start with basics: 'It's about a man who…'. At the same time, never be afraid to take a chance on an imaginative or risky interpretation of an ambiguous phrase or image. When writing about poetry, ambiguity is not a block to understanding but a key to it. It's *supposed* to be difficult, remember? So explain how it's difficult. For bonus points, call those difficult bits 'problematic'. Most of all, consider *why* the poet wanted you to puzzle over that particular phrase. How does this part's difficulty contribute to the whole?

When you first read a poem, read it ten times. Always, always, you start to notice things. Strange intonations. Bits that don't quite work rhythmically. Half rhymes that both reinforce (because they sound sort-of similar) and reject (the sounds don't quite match) the link between two words that might sound alike but, here, point in opposite directions.

The ten questions

For each of those ten reads, try thinking about a different aspect of it. The below list is by no means a binding obligation – see where the poem takes you. But it is based on 25 years' experience of answering very difficult exam questions. So here are the ten questions to consider as you read a poem:

1. What's it about? *Content*

2. Is there alliteration? *Form*

3. Is there rhyme? *Form*

4. What is the rhythm like? *Form*

5. How does its lineation work? Are there stanzas? *Form*

6. Are there any metaphors and similes? *Form*

7. What does the poet's word choice tell you? *Form*

8. Who is the narrator; who is the main character? *Form*

9. What is the poem's mood and tone? *Form*

10. What's it *really* about? *Content & Form*

Now we can test this theory on two poems by Philip Larkin. Why Philip Larkin? Because in my opinion he's the greatest poet to write in English in the last two hundred years. Please read each one ten times, considering a different one of the ten questions each time. Make your own notes on the page. Then consider what my own annotations mean, which I've numbered using the ten questions so you can see which technique I'm referring to. You'll notice I've focused on only one or two aspects of form in each poem. That's because I think they're the key to understanding it, and answering the biggest question about any poem: what's it *really* about?

Water

If I were called in[7]
To construct a religion
I should make use of water.
Going to church
Would entail a fording[7]
To dry, different clothes;
My liturgy[7] would employ
Images of sousing,
A furious devout[7] drench,
And I should raise in the east
A glass of water
Where any-angled[7] light
Would congregate[7] endlessly.

1. What's it about?
2. Alliteration
3. Rhyme
4. Rhythm
5. Lineation and stanzas
6. Metaphors and similes
7. Word choice
8. Narrator and character
9. Mood and tone
10. What's it *really* about?

1. What's it about? The guy likes water so much he wants to marry it, or worship it, or something. We get it. Water is life. We're 60% water, the Earth is 70% covered with water, and we'd die without it; every major world city is either a port or has a river running through it. You could answer this question – what's it about? – by simply quoting the first stanza:

If I were called in
To construct a religion
I should make use of water.

But is that all there is to this poem?

7. Word Choice. All the words marked refer to religious practices, especially of baptism, in which a new Christian's sins are symbolically washed away (a ford is a crossing at a river where it is shallow enough to walk across, like the point in the River Jordan where John the Baptist met Jesus Christ and baptised him). And the facing east while worshipping perhaps makes us think of European Muslims facing east when they pray to Mecca, their holy city in Saudi Arabia. Larkin has thoroughly grounded his proposed new religion in the language of old ones. Why has he done this? Is he just copying these two already successful world religions (there are seven billion people in the world – 1.5 billion are Muslim and 1.5 billion are Christian)?

No. He isn't just copying. Look at the words marked. That 'any-angled' light shining through the glass suggests Larkin is thinking of the way light travels through glass and water differently than it travels through air – they all refract (break up) light in different ways. Those angles make us think of science, not religion, and that is exactly what Larkin wants.

And why on earth would this unassuming poet be 'called in/ To construct a religion'? Jesus and Mohammed were not *called in*; they were prophets, inspired by God to set down His wishes for His people. To be *called in* to do so makes the foundation of a great world religion sound like a boring office job. 'Hello Mr Christ, we've booked meeting room C for you but we'll need you out by 11:30 I'm afraid' – this is not a sentence that appears anywhere in the King James Bible. So why is Larkin trying to make religion sound boring and humdrum?

10. What's it *really* about? Because he's attacking it, that's why. Larkin doesn't believe any of these Bronze Age myths. Look at the opening line:

> If I were called in
> To construct a religion…

Well, according to most religions' foundational texts, they were founded on clear, detailed instructions that came, via their chosen prophets, straight from God. No construction necessary. But in that word 'construct' Larkin strongly suggests there is something man-made, or made-up, about religions. That they are not the literal word of God. That religions can be and have been just whisked up out of nothing more than human ingenuity, and that they are therefore no more true than fairy tales.

Larkin wrote this poem in 1954, after the American L. Ron Hubbard had published his 1950 book *Dianetics*, which founded a new religious movement called Scientology, which many in the West follow (including several Hollywood film stars). Hubbard is also recorded as saying earlier that 'The quickest way to make a million dollars is to invent a religion.' Larkin is suggesting – and as an agnostic I couldn't say if he's right or wrong – that all religions are *constructed* and therefore man-made, and therefore false.

That's a long way from our first response to it – that here's a guy who just really likes water. And that's why you have to read a poem more than once: you have to look at it from every possible angle, to look beneath the surface to see which techniques the poet is using to convey the hidden subtext of what he's *really* saying.

And so, on to poem two:

The Mower

The mower stalled, twice; kneeling, I found
A hedgehog jammed up against the blades,
Killed. It had been in the long grass.

I had seen it before, and even fed it, once.[4]
Now I had mauled its unobtrusive world
Unmendably. Burial was no help:

Next morning I got up and it did not.
The first day after a death, the new absence
Is always the same; we should be careful

Of each other, we should be kind
While there is still time.[10]

1. What's it about?
2. Alliteration
3. Rhyme
4. Rhythm
5. Lineation and stanzas
6. Metaphors and similes
7. Word Choice
8. Narrator and character
9. Mood and Tone
10. What's it *really* about?

1. A man accidentally kills a hedgehog[13] with his lawnmower and regrets it.

4.

x x /	x x /	x /	x /	x /
I had seen	it before,	and e-	-ven fed	it, once.

Because a line's stresses are more important than its unstressed syllables, like the tentpoles a tent's roof is strung across, we tend to focus on them when assessing that line's rhythm. This line is two anapaests (two short or unstressed syllables followed by one long or stressed syllable)

x x /

followed by three iambs

x /

which is sort-of regular, sort-of irregular, starting slow and solemn, then speeding up in its second half: the poet is perhaps cheering up a bit as he remembers that nice thing he did once for the unlucky hedgehog. Except the line becomes slow and solemn again at the very end. And even though it ends with three iambs – the usually jaunty, sing-song, reliable iamb, that goes te-TUM te-TUM te-TUM – the line ends as

[13] Related fact – hedgehogs sometimes crawl into bonfires for shelter overnight and die when they are lit, so burn your bonfires as soon as possible after building them.

slowly and sadly as it started, because of that second comma that breaks the last iamb in half, and slows everything down again.

So let's talk about punctuation instead. How is it that the addition of the second comma makes this line so much more mournful?

I had seen it before, and even fed it, once.

It's because that word 'once' can mean both 'one time' (he only fed it one time out of the several times he saw it), and also it can mean 'in the past' (as in 'once upon a time, and never again after that'), with the heavy implication that the hedgehog is dead.

What would removing that second comma do to the meaning of the line?

I had seen it before, and even fed it once.

The line – though still ambiguous – would carry the former meaning: 'I fed it on one occasion'. But the pause after 'it' and before 'once' certainly brings us to the latter meaning, the more regretful one, which is the one we hear.

'I even fed it once' is more cheery, recalling a kind deed done for the hedgehog. But cheeriness isn't appropriate in these circumstances. Someone is dead. So when the remorseful poet says that he 'even fed it, once', it means that the one kindness he did for this unobtrusive little animal was also the last. The mournful pause created by the comma tells us that the hedgehog existed once and once only, in the past, and that it can't now have a saucer of milk set out for it last thing before the poet goes to bed.

It's probably the saddest moment in a very sad poem and it's all because of that comma. Poetry is a spoken form, and it matters where you pause for breath. Punctuation matters. Form matters.

10. There are two kinds of empathy: emotional empathy, where you feel what the other person or creature is feeling, as in lines five-six, where the poet feels the hedgehog's pain:

> Now I had mauled its unobtrusive world
> Unmendably.

And there is also cognitive empathy, where you think about what the other person is feeling, and make an informed guess. You're reading their mind, really. At the end of the poem, having thoroughly softened us up, Larkin tells us what he really means. He knows we're upset about the dead hedgehog: he's thought about what we're feeling, and made an informed guess. Then he makes a switch. He knows we're feeling sad about this small animal dying – which we can't do anything about – and he manipulates us into considering the wider point about not harming others. He's really talking about people, not hedgehogs, and the enjambment after 'careful' does the work of deftly changing the subject:

> we should be careful
> Of each other, we should be kind
> While there is still time.

It's a simple but resonant reiteration of the Golden Rule – do unto others as you would have them do to you – which, like the very short and readable *Animal Farm*, employs the traditional English sentimentality about not hurting animals in order to make us think about not hurting our fellow human beings. It's also a reminder ('While there is still time') that we're all going to die, and that one day, all that will be left of us are the memories of how we treated the people who loved us while we were alive.

'Afterwards'

Philip Larkin's favourite poet was Thomas Hardy, whose poem 'Afterwards' imagines the beauty of the spring that will inevitably arrive after his own equally inevitable death.

He wonders how he will be remembered by those who knew him:

> When the Present has latched its postern behind my tremulous stay,
> And the May month flaps its glad green leaves like wings,
> Delicate-filmed as new-spun silk, will the neighbours say,
> 'He was a man who used to notice such things'?

My final advice for your English exam, and for your life after it, is that you too become such a person.

FOURTH QUESTION

THE PRISONER'S DILEMMA

Okay, so you're a bank robber and you've been caught, and so has someone else in your gang. Bad luck. They're keeping you in separate rooms so you can't communicate, but you know your buddy is somewhere in the same police station as you. The detective interrogating you offers a deal. If you rat on your buddy, you can go free, he'll get ten years' hard time. If you keep quiet, you'll get one year in prison. What would you rather do? One year in jail, or none? How much do you like your buddy? How much is loyalty worth?

Then it occurs to you. Your buddy is somewhere in the same police station, being offered the same deal. If he turns you in, he goes free. If he stays quiet, he gets a year of jail time. So you're pretty sure your buddy is having the same thought. Does he turn you in and go free? Or does he keep quiet and do a year in jail?

There's one more thing. If you both turn each other in, you both get ten years. That's what your interrogators are hoping – that there's no honour among thieves, as the saying goes. So what do you do? Do you keep quiet, hoping he does too, and you both do a year inside? A year isn't that long, is it? Or do you rat on the guy, hoping he doesn't do the same, and go free that day? Unless he has the same idea, in which case you're both looking down the barrel of ten years' hard time.

What do you do?

7

HOW TO AVOID COMMON MISTAKES

Everyone makes mistakes, and different people often make the same ones. This final chapter is likely to be the most widely useful in the book. It will detail common mistakes I've seen my students make during my 20 years of tutoring, then outline the straightforward fixes that worked for them.

That said, what I'm not going to do is give you a series of rules that you'll expend energy trying to learn, and more energy worrying that you've forgotten. These are only a collection of the ones I find most interesting...

It's/Its – not unusual

It's = It is, a verb. The second 'i' is missed out in its abbreviation. The apostrophe is there to show where the 'i' would have gone.

Its = Of it, a possessive pronoun that works like an adjective that agrees with the noun. No apostrophe is used because no letter is missed out – it's just a different form of the word

'It', that means 'Of it', in the same way that 'I' and 'my' are different forms, with different meanings, of the same word. In Latin it would be called the genitive case.

When you're not sure which one to use, try writing it out both ways. Substituting the 'It's'/ 'Its' in your sentence with both possibilities, one after the other, will help your system one thinking (aka your intuition, aka the 'thinking without thinking' you do all the time without really noticing), and help you to decide which version is the one you want here, based on the thousands of times you've seen it written correctly, and which you've subconsciously stored somewhere in your brain. The syntax of your sentence will break down very obviously if you use an 'It is' – from the verb 'to be' – where an 'Of it' – possessive pronoun – is required, or vice versa. ~~Of it not so difficult!~~ It is not so difficult!

	The verb 'to be'	What it means	The possessive pronoun	What it means
1st person singular	I'm	= *I am*	my	= *of me*
2nd person singular	you're	= *you are*	your	= *of you*
3rd person singular	he's	= *he is*	his	= *of him*
	she's	= *she is*	her	= *of her*
	it's	**= *it is***	**its**	**= *of it***

1st person plural	we're	= *we are*	our	= *of us*
2nd person plural	you're	= *you are*	your	= *of you*
3rd person plural	they're	= *they are*	their	= *of them*

Oi!

Hoi polloi, never the hoi polloi. Why? Because 'hoi', or oi, is already the Ancient Greek word for 'the'. So saying 'the hoi polloi' means 'the the many'. As it's used in English today, the phrase 'hoi polloi' generally means 'the majority of people, whom I think I'm better than, because I know a phrase in Ancient Greek that describes them which they wouldn't understand'. But if you say 'the hoi polloi', it means that you don't understand this Ancient Greek phrase either, the one you're using to belittle them, which means you're actually no better than them: in fact you're worse, because you're trying to belittle them without any good reason.

Similar, but rarer, and not nearly as bad – because people don't use it snobbishly to assert themselves over other people – is another common mistake. The Ancient Greek word 'nous', usually pronounced to rhyme with 'house', means 'mind', and has come in English to mean 'common sense'. But actually the word 'nous' in Ancient Greek is pronounced 'noose'. So people talking about their own or others' 'nous' are actually showing their ignorance rather than their 'common sense'. The Ancient Greek word 'naus', meaning 'ship', from which we get the word 'nautical', is the one we should be pronouncing to rhyme with 'house' – and not 'nous', which should rhyme with 'noose'.

Less money, fewer problems

In his posthumously released 1997 song 'Mo Money Mo Problems', the multi-millionaire rapper Notorious B.I.G. complains that becoming wealthier just makes life more complicated: more money, more problems. The logical corollary of that statement is that less money means less problems. But there's something about that second statement that doesn't sound quite right, isn't there? And it's not just the counterintuitive idea that being poorer means an easier life. Less money, less problems? Quite apart from the idea they express, those words sound jarring, don't they? Any idea why?

It's because 'more' is an adjective that can refer to both singular ('money') and plural nouns ('problems'). But the opposite of 'more' can be two words: 'less' (when it refers to a singular noun, like 'money'), and 'fewer' (when it refers to a plural noun, like 'problems'). It's pretty easy to spot plural nouns – they nearly always end in an 's'. So it should have been 'less money, fewer problems'.

Similarly, the word 'right' has two antonyms (opposites), depending on the sense that 'right' is being used in, as in the children's favourite logical trap 'Are you all right?' 'Yes.' 'I'm not. I'm half left'.

Logical fallacies

It is usually a mistake to attribute to malicious intent what can have the more simple explanation of human accident, human incompetence or human stupidity. This is the principle of Occam's Razor, which we saw earlier, a metaphorical blade that slices away the extraneous, superfluous elements from an explanation, to leave only the simplest and therefore likeliest one:

- 'Tony hasn't got his homework.'
- 'Maybe his dog ate it.'
- 'No, he probably just didn't do it.' Occam's Razor.

The former England striker Gary Lineker would always shoot for goal instead of pass to a team-mate, because, he said, if he shoots, he might score or he might not – toss a coin, hope for heads; but if he passes the ball – toss a coin – it might get cut out by a defender. And *even then* if his team-mate does manage to shoot, well, you have to toss another coin. The chance of a coin toss coming up heads is ½, but the chance of two heads in a row is ½ x ½ = ¼. Half as likely to score if he passes. Simplest solution usually the best. Shoot, Gary.

On the other hand, asking yourself *cui bono?* – literally, 'to whose good' is this happening, who benefits from this turn of events? – is one of the most useful questions a historian has in his armoury.

A variant of this is 'Follow the money': large-scale nefarious deeds require the bribery or payment of large numbers of people, which leaves a paper trail – evidence – that can link and eventually condemn the malefactors. Terrorists were often caught this way before the advent of mobile phones, whose signal, and hence their owner's location, is easily and instantly traceable.

The phrase 'Follow the money' originates with the *Washington Post* journalists Woodward and Bernstein, who were advised by their secret source 'Deep Throat' to do just that: thereby uncovering the Republican President Nixon's use of phone tapping and other espionage against the opposition Democrat party, which led to his impeachment by the two houses of Congress, and eventually to his resignation.

Accusatives – A brief introduction to Latin

Most people understand the difference between the following two questions, until it comes time for them to use one in a sentence.

> When you've done that lab report, can you send it to Bill and I?

The sentence above is actually wrong, as proper as it sounds. Try taking Bill out of that sentence – it sounds weird, right? You would never ask someone to send something to 'I' when he or she is done. The reason it sounds weird is because 'I' is the object of that sentence – and 'I' should not be used in objects. In that situation, you'd use 'me.'

> When you've done that lab report, can you send it to Bill and me?

Much better. That's because I and me, while they're the same person (me, myself and I), they are different forms of the same pronoun. Whether you use I or me depends on whether it is I (nominative, subject) who is doing the verb, or having the verb done to me (accusative, object).

> Bill and I need that lab report when you've done it. (Correct)
>
> Bill and me need that lab report when you've done it. (Wrong)

My first hour with a new Latinist is spent moving two (one English, one Latin) nouns (**nominative**, which I will mark in **bold**) and two (one English, one Latin) nouns (*accusative*, which I will mark in *italics*) around two stuck-down verbs, trying out the two possible word orders. That relationship, between the noun who is doing the verb (**Subject**), and the noun to whom it is being done (*Object*) is conceptually unfamiliar to us with our largely uninflected language, and yet of crucial, foundational importance.

- **Canis** *hominem* mordet
- *Hominem* **canis** mordet

translate as:

- **Dog** bites *man*
- **Dog** bites *man*

and likewise:

- **Homo** *canem* mordet
- *Canem* **homo** mordet

both mean:

- **Man** bites *dog*
- **Man** bites *dog*

Why? Because Latin is an *inflected* language and English, by and large, is not. The endings of our words rarely change, apart from the -s we add to singular nouns to make them plural, or the –'s that we add to nouns to make them *possessives*: *Dave's* car means the car *of Dave*, both examples of what in Latin nouns (and, unlike English, adjectives) is called the *genitive* case. Finally there's the extra -s English adds to the third person singular of present tense verbs:

SINGULAR		
1st person	I	bite
		mordeo
2nd person	you	bite
		mordes
3rd person	he, she or it	**bites**
		mordet
PLURAL		
1st person	we	bite
		mordemus
2nd person	you	bite
		mordetis
3rd person	they	bite
		mordent

So English nouns and adjectives don't *decline*, and our verbs don't *conjugate*, like Latin ones. Latin sentences, like the mathematical functions plus and multiply, are *commutative*, giving the same result whichever order they are written in. English is *non-commutative*, like subtract and divide. Our sentences depend far more on *word order* than on inflection to indicate the person *who* acts as the *subject* of the verb, and *whom* the verb makes its *object*.

But our pronouns *do* decline, coming as they do from another (semi-)inflected extinct European language, Old High German. And pushing around another set of flash cards, pronouns this time, can help us appreciate the versatility of Latin's many inflections (ten each for nouns, 30 each for adjectives and 106 different possible endings, and hence meanings, for each and every Latin verb[14]). The many different suffixes bolted onto the end of most of Latin's words completely change their meaning and role in the sentence.

At first there seems to be the same problem with English pronouns as with English nouns, but worse – switching them around doesn't invert the meaning; it makes the sentences meaningless:

- **is** *eam* amat (okay)
- *eam* **is** amat (okay)

become

- **He** likes *her* (okay)
- *Her* likes **he** (not okay)

And, with the nominative feminine pronoun *ea*, or she, used as the subject, and the accusative masculine pronoun *eum*, or him:

[14] According to Nicholas Ostler's fine history of Latin, *ad infinitum*.

- **ea** *eum* amat (okay)
- *eum* **ea** amat (okay)

both mean

- **She** likes *him* (okay)
- *Him* likes **she** (not okay)

What if we make a small change and put the verb at the end of the English sentences, though? We're still flipping the order of the pronouns, which when we did it with the nouns also turned around the meaning of the sentence. This time, we can see how inflections, the two variants of a word (he/him), and likewise of (she/her), make it possible in one small corner of English to construct a sentence whose meaning does not depend entirely on its word order. This is how every single Latin sentence works, and it's the first thing you'll need to get your head around. So here goes:

- *He* likes **her** (okay)
- **Her** *he* likes (okay!)

'He doesn't like most people, but her he likes.' That works, doesn't it, even though the words are reversed? It's roughly the same meaning as 'he likes her' even with the pronouns transposed. It's still 'he' as the subject of the verb 'likes', and 'her' as the object of the liking.

Likewise:

- **She** likes *him* (okay)
- *Him* **she** likes (okay!)

'Her contempt for the rest of humanity is absolute, but *him* she likes.' Bad luck for the rest of humanity, but it's still 'her' as the subject and 'him' as the object.

In all these card-shunting exercises the purpose is to muddle the monoglot student's innate sense of how his or her own language works, and to physically prove for themselves that there's something very different about this new (very old) one – Latin. Anyone can see which English versions are right and which ones are wrong. But when you ask them to explain why, there is a pause. That moment, for the majority of fledgling Latinists, is the first time they have had to think deeply about how language, particularly their own native language – let alone this strange dead beast of one – really works. That insight into one's own language, and language generally, as being a non-neutral codification of the culture in which it arose, and all the other insights that follow it, are why Latin is worth studying. That and the poetry, the best of which, to my mind, knocks Shakespeare into a cocked hat.

Exam technique (and The Meaning of Life)

When you're an adult, the thing that will seem like the most important thing in life, the thing you can't get enough of, even if you already have plenty of it, is money. (Actually things like love and friendship and fun are just as important, if not more so, but you're not stupid; you probably already knew that.)

At school, though, and especially in an exam, there's nothing remotely as important as marks. Examiners don't let you forget it, either. Next to every single question you have to answer, usually by the right hand margin, is a little number in brackets telling you how many marks are available for this question.

This is important information. The marks available for a question tell you how long you should spend answering it: a rule of thumb is to divide the marks available for this question by the total marks available in the whole exam. That fraction will tell you roughly what fraction of the total time available in the exam you should spend on this particular part of it. Of course you will need to spend time reading the question, reading any text that the question might be based on, and thinking about your answer – this might mean spending more time than your calculation suggests. That's fine. If there are lots of additional questions attached to, or perhaps even dependent on your answer to this first one, maybe called things like (b) or (ii) or (b) (i), then it might be worth spending more time on part (a), because skipping the first bit might mean missing out not just on (3) marks but on (3) + (1) + (2) + (4) marks if it's a four-part question that you can't complete without working out part (a).

Here are a couple of exam questions of my own devising:

1. What is the volume of a room 2m high, 75cm deep, and 80cm wide? (30)
2. What is the meaning of life? (3)

The mark scheme doesn't only tell you roughly *how long* to spend answering each question, it also tells you *how* to answer it. Now, clearly, I've got the mark scheme the wrong way around. Question one is pretty easy and only involves converting two of those dimensions into metres (0.75m and 0.8m), and then multiplying all three numbers together. It's only two pieces of work, really, so even three marks – let alone 30 – would be generous. Some exams would only offer two marks for what is really only two pieces of work. It certainly pays to be suspicious if a Maths question offers a lot of marks for only a few, and quite easy, calculations: *maybe you've missed something*. In exams, as in life, there is no such thing as a free lunch.

Likewise, question two is not many marks for quite a lot of thinking. The meaning of life is a big question, one you can't really answer until it's over, and by then (if you believe Richard Dawkins), it's too late for anything, because you're totally dead for ever with no afterlife or reincarnation or anything. No one has definitively, completely answered this question, and people have been trying for thousands of years, so three marks seems on the stingy side; even 30 marks aren't really a sufficient reward for a perfect answer, one that would transform seven billion people's lives overnight.

But you've got to play the hand you're dealt. So, if I had to give an answer for question 1 I'd certainly start with 2m x 0.75m x 0.8m = 1.2m^3. So that's three marks. What about the other 27?

Well, I'd start off by asking, on paper, what kind of room this is. In a 30-mark question, which most likely needs answering in an essay, asking rhetorical questions is a good way of getting marks from your examiner, and ideas from yourself, which lead on to more marks. Apart from the caves painted by our prehistoric ancestors or inhabited by religious hermits, all rooms are man-made. And all naturally-formed caves have very irregular shapes, unlike this room which is a perfect cuboid. So it's not a cave. Most rooms are made not only *by* humans, but also *for* humans. But this room is tiny, no use as a bedroom, a study, or anything else. You couldn't even sit down in it. Perhaps it's a doll's house, but then why is it so high – its only really human dimension? Perhaps it's a cupboard, but the question title refers to 'a room', and a cupboard is not a room – it's a different category, and a room is for living in, not storing things. Perhaps it's a toilet, but it would only be of limited use if it prevented sitting, and the lack of space for air to circulate would make the smell terrible. So why (I can feel another rhetorical question coming on) would someone deliberately build a room that would be so unpleasantly claustrophobic and physically uncomfortable to spend any time in?

I can only think of two possible answers to that last question: one of them is unpleasant, and the other is very unpleasant. In the century or two after Henry VIII forcibly converted English Christians from their allegiance to the Catholic Church in Rome, to his new Protestant Church of England, many devoted Catholics continued, in secret, to worship in the old way. Rich Catholic families would pay, support and, when necessary, hide Catholic priests, in order to have them perform clandestine services in their homes. These homes, more like castles really, had very thick walls, perhaps a meter thick in places. And within these walls, or beside them and disguised by the thickness, they would create tiny hollow spaces, called priest holes, so that these renegade churchmen could hide in them if a suspicious sheriff came calling during the forbidden service. Discovery often meant being burned at the stake as a heretic: in the great old houses of England there are many of these priest holes, and perhaps many more yet undiscovered. So, this inhumanly-small room could have been for humans after all, to hide in from an inhuman fate.

There is a worse possibility, and it is this: perhaps it was built deliberately small in order to punish, or torture, the person inside. The Tower of London, built by William I in the years after 1066, and extended by subsequent monarchs over the next three centuries, contained a tiny cell called 'Little Ease' built for just this purpose. In the 20th century, both Stalin in his gulag archipelago, and Hitler in the concentration camps of Oranienburg and Dachau, and the concentration and extermination camp of Auschwitz, built and used these cells to torture and punish their many enemies. In 2012 the American soldier Chelsea Manning, imprisoned for making public through Wikileaks hundreds of thousands of documents that showed crimes committed by the United States military over the past two decades, claimed that she had been kept for two months in a cell of similarly tiny dimensions. So, many such tiny cells have been built and used for this dread purpose over (at least) the last millennium. Perhaps question 1 refers to one of these rooms.

It may not have been pleasant, but I think we've had a good go at squeezing as many of the 30 available marks out of this question. There's *always* something else to say. In an exam the only acceptable excuse for putting your pen down, or (because the thinking and planning bit is more important than the writing bit) for disengaging your brain, is if the invigilator tells you to.

The other question presents the opposite problem. What

is the meaning of life? How should you answer a seemingly huge question in the very short time that the mark scheme tells you to spend on it? It's just three marks, out of the 40, 50, or 100 available, and you simply *must* spend nearly all of your *preciously short* 60, 90, or 120 minutes elsewhere, if you are to get an 'A' on this paper to go with all the other 'A's you'll need to win this damn scholarship.

Your answer must be brief. And so will mine (ish). It's really an essay question, which requires a personal answer bolstered by an argument and supporting evidence that considers more than one point of view. But there's not really any time for any of that, so my answer would lean on the words and thoughts of eight other people instead.

The Meaning of Life is a Monty Python film at whose end, after ninety minutes of largely unrelated messing around, someone is handed an envelope containing the meaning of life, which turns out to be:

> Try and be nice to people, avoid getting fat, read a good book every now and then, get some walking in, and try to live together in peace and harmony with people of all creeds and nations.

In *The Life of Brian*, another Python film, the unwilling messiah Brian Cohen wakes to find a huge crowd of followers gathered outside his house and tries thusly to get rid of them:

> Look, you've got it all wrong! You don't NEED to follow ME, you don't NEED to follow ANYBODY! You've all got to think for yourselves! You're ALL individuals!

Both speeches, in two pretty absurd films, are actually pretty good advice. For total absurdity, which is what this question seems to ask for (you've got three minutes to answer a question that 100 billion humans have failed to answer in 100,000 years), we might turn to Douglas Adams's satirical space travel masterpiece *The Hitchhiker's Guide to the Galaxy.* Super-intelligent inter-dimensional beings have built a supercomputer the size of a city called Deep Thought precisely to answer this question and, after 7.5 million years of calculations it is finally ready with the definitive and final answer, which turns out to be:

> 42.

But my favourite, non-silly answer to the 'Meaning of Life' question was written in 1947 by a proto-hippie who lived in a tent under the Hollywood sign in Los Angeles. He was called Eden Ahbez and the song is called 'Nature Boy':

> The greatest thing you'll ever learn
> Is just to love and be loved in return.

An exam mark scheme is a delicately-posed instrument of interrogation that, if you read it closely enough, will tell you exactly how to direct the scope of your thoughts, the exact form your answer should take, and finally the length at which you should write it.

Last word on grammar

Only worry about acquiring grammatical habits that you believe make useful distinctions. Split infinitives (to boldly go) are a meaningless hangover from a time when grammarians wanted to make English like Latin. On the other hand, I think the difference between 'I' and 'me' is worth the hassle – because it tells you who's the active person in the sentence. English – Globish – is changing. It's up to anyone who uses the language to cleave to the useful stuff, and forget the rest.

THE PRISONER'S DILEMMA

Answer

Okay, so I lied to you. The scenario I presented you with isn't really based on two bank robbers deciding whether or not to rat on each other. You probably think I presented the question this way, in a compelling, conflict-heavy scenario, to make it seem more real, more scary, and that really this question, this 'thought experiment', was designed to explain human behaviour in some abstract or uninteresting way. Maybe you think it has to do with how people behave in queues, or how they choose which kind of car to buy.

If only that were so. In reality, The Prisoner's Dilemma was a game invented at the RAND Corporation, an American military research institute, in 1950, one year after the Soviet Union had developed a nuclear bomb, and five years after America had dropped two such bombs on Hiroshima and Nagasaki. It was the beginning of the Cold War between these two countries, which is generally thought to have ended with the collapse of the Soviet Union in 1991, but which has never really ended, because both countries still have the power to destroy each other utterly, and the world with it – and over the years they have been joined by other nuclear powers including China, Britain, France, Israel, India, Pakistan and North Korea.

This game, the Prisoner's Dilemma, was invented as a way of thinking about a possible nuclear war between America and the Soviet Union. It was thought that a surprise nuclear attack on one country by another would be so devastating that the other country would not be able to respond, like the betrayal of one bank robber by another which he'd only discover when it was too late to retaliate. So in this version of the game each player has only one turn, and both are played simultaneously, so neither player has any information about the other player's behaviour to help inform their decision.

Final thought: as I write this in early 2018, the hands of the Doomsday Clock are at Two Minutes to Midnight. This is a theoretical measure, administered by the Bulletin of the Atomic Scientists, of how close the World is to nuclear war. Midnight means means that nuclear war is inevitable. We are as close to Midnight as we have ever been since the Doomsday Clock was instigated, following the annihilation of Hiroshima and Nagasaki in 1945.

The original Prisoner's Dilemma is a thought experiment that was developed by RAND employees Merrill Flood and Melvin Dresher in order to contemplate, and thereby minimise, the risk of nuclear war. And it may well have done so – it hasn't happened yet, after all. But the person who was commemorated in London in 2017 as having made 'perhaps the single most valuable contribution to human survival in modern history' made that contribution based on a personal hunch rather than any considered logical strategy.

His name was Vasili Arkhipov and he was the third officer on a nuclear-armed submarine during the Cuban Missile Crisis of 1962, a 13-day stand-off between Russian and

American navies, when his captain, along with the second officer, believed that a depth charge that had exploded near the submarine meant that they were under attack from an American warship. The captain and his second officer prepared to fire back with a nuclear missile that would almost certainly have been the opening salvo of a global apocalypse. But launching the missile required the agreement of the three senior officers on board and Arkhipov, as third officer, refused to launch, despite considerable pressure from his two senior officers, because he felt, correctly, that the American depth charge was a warning shot rather than an attack.

That day in 1962, Vasili Arkhipov played the single-turn Prisoner's Dilemma game. In fact, unlike the theoretical version of the game invented at the RAND Corporation, Arkhipov did have some kind of idea of how his opponent in the game was going to use his turn. Sitting in his small enclosed cell hundreds of metres underwater, he saw the evidence as pointing to an opponent who might very possibly have already chosen to default, or betray, or attack, with devastating results for Arkhipov's side. And yet, based on nothing more than a hunch, Arkhipov chose to cooperate, to keep the peace, to refuse to launch. And in making that decision, one surely based on instinct and emotion as much as logic, Vasili Arkhipov prevented nuclear war, and quite literally saved the world. In purely numerical terms, given the billions of lives he saved, Vasili Arkhipov is the greatest hero in the history of humanity, although the continuing existence of nuclear weapons in the world may call for another such hero in the future. Let's hope not.

I suppose, if there's a lesson here, it's that all these thought experiments that try to model human behaviour are just that – models, which always simplify and distort a more complex reality – and that it's very difficult to predict how we would respond in a real situation like that, let alone how an enemy would. Certainly, instinct and emotion might play a larger part than these logic-based models would suggest. On the basis of Vasili Arkhipov's example, thank God for that. Here's a picture of him.

P.S.

On not forgetting

'It's strange what you don't forget,' as Jayne Anne Phillips's 1984 novel *Machine Dreams* strangely, and unforgettably begins.

What, honestly, do you think you'll remember of this book in ten years' time? A couple of things? Maybe three or four things? In which case, I think I've done my job. Of all the books I listed in my first chapter, I honestly don't remember a great deal, especially because two or three decades have passed since I read most of them. I do remember that I enjoyed them, which is why I've recommended them to you, but almost everything else is a blur.

You may have already forgotten everything I've just said. So it goes. Forgetting is inevitable, memory being what it is. Trust your brain to retain the things you need. And it's fine, because there was another purpose to this book.

If a book is a kind of papery distillation of the person who wrote it, and I think it is or I wouldn't have said it, then I hope this one has made you feel a particular way. I hope you feel confident. Confident that there are interesting things in the world, things worth knowing for no other reason than that they're interesting, and that you can know them if you want to; and finally that – believe it or not – some of this stuff can even be fun.

ACKNOWLEDGEMENTS

Thanks to my agent, Piers Blofeld, who was the first person to think this book was a good idea, and to Gaia Banks and everyone at Sheil Land. Thanks to my editor, Helena Sutcliffe, for her deft mind and eye, to Aurea Carpenter and Rebecca Nicolson, and all at Short Books. Thanks to George Norman for the drawings, and to Two Associates for the cover design.

Thanks to my critical readers, Josh Adeyemi, Hassan Azad, Thomas Avery, Jamie Bartlett, James Bickford-Smith, Nina Blychert Wisnia, Celia Bowie, Elliot Cannell, Bill Cannon, Phoebe Cronk, Olga Danylyuk, Linda Davis, Edward Dick, Madeleine Feeny, Elena Gorokhova, Sue Hall, Susannah Hamilton, Samuel Johnston, Susanna Johnston, Kate Cronk, Lorraine McConachie, Barbara McKinnon, Megan Meshiea, Thirumalai Naicker, Julia Norman, Oliver Norman, Neepa Patel, Kate Potel, Abi Rana, Marina Smith, Paul Turner, Alice Wallther and Anna Zelkina.

Especial thanks to Charles Bonas, Jeremy Catto, Walter Oakeshott and Margaret Thatcher.

Thanks to the many wonderful teachers I've had in my life, including but not limited to Mr Anderson, Mrs Ashcroft,

Miss Butler, Miss Cannon, Dr Cattermole, Dr Cramer, Mr Crick, Miss Dugdale, Miss Edge, Mr Farmer, Mr Fraser, Dr Gregory (Mrs), Mr Hewitson, Mrs Howarth, Mr Johnson, Mr MacDonald, Mr McKinnon (L), Mr McKinnon (N), Mr Nevin, Miss Ovenden, Mr Raybould, Mr Roberts, Mr Robertson, Mr Shelley, Mrs Shepherd, Mr Taylor, Mrs Tyldesley, Mr Vear, Mr Wallis, Mr Williams, Mr Winkley, and Mr Wyke.

Thanks to Phoebe and Madeleine for their love and support.

And finally thanks to the many outstanding students I've had the good luck to tutor, whose contribution to the writing of this book, they might be surprised to learn, has been immeasurable.

ABOUT THE AUTHOR

Joe Norman has been a tutor of children aged 10-13 since 2000. He specialises in training children for entrance and scholarships to top schools such as Eton, Winchester and Westminster. He studied at Winchester College and Oxford University.